WALKING - - - - →
AUSTIN

 **WILDERNESS PRESS** . . . *on the trail since 1967*

WALKING ----->
AUSTIN

33 Walking Tours Exploring Historical Legacies, Musical Culture, and Abundant Natural Beauty

Charlie Llewellin

 WILDERNESS PRESS *... on the trail since 1967*

Walking Austin: 33 Walking Tours Exploring Historical Legacies, Musical Culture, and Abundant Natural Beauty

First edition, first printing
Copyright © 2019 by Charlie Llewellin

Library of Congress Cataloging-in-Publication Data

Names: Llewellin, Charlie, 1959- author.
Title: Walking Austin : 33 walking tours exploring historical legacies, musical culture, and abundant natural beauty / Charles Llewellin.
Description: Birmingham, AL : Wilderness Press, 2019. | Includes index.
Identifiers: LCCN 2019001158 | ISBN 9780899979533 (pbk.)
Subjects: LCSH: Austin (Tex.)—Guidebooks. | Walking—Texas—Austin—Guidebooks. | Historic buildings—Texas—Galveston—Guidebooks. | Austin (Tex.)—Buildings, structures, etc.—Guidebooks.
Classification: LCC F394.A93 L54 2019 | DDC 917.64/3104—dc23
LC record available at https://lccn.loc.gov/2019001158

Published by   🦬 **WILDERNESS PRESS**
An imprint of AdventureKEEN
2204 First Ave. S., Suite 102
Birmingham, AL 35233
800-443-7227, fax 205-326-1012
wildernesspress.com

Visit wildernesspress.com for a complete listing of our books and for ordering information. Contact us at our website, at facebook.com/wildernesspress1967, or at twitter.com/wilderness1967 with questions or comments. To find out more about who we are and what we're doing, visit blog.wildernesspress.com.

Frontispiece: Charles Umlauf's *The Kiss* (1970) at Umlauf Sculpture Garden (see Walk 31, page 166).

Cover photo: Lucy in Disguise with Diamonds on South Congress Avenue (see Walk 27, page 141). © Art Anderson (CC BY-SA 3.0 [https://creativecommons.org/licenses/by-sa/3.0]), via Wikimedia Commons

Project editor: Kate Johnson
Maps: Scott McGrew
Cover and interior design: Jonathan Norberg
Interior photos: Charlie Llewellin
Proofreader: Rebecca Henderson
Indexer: Rich Carlson

Manufactured in the United States of America
Distributed by Publishers Group West

SAFETY NOTICE: Although Wilderness Press and the author have made every attempt to ensure that the information in this book is accurate at press time, they are not responsible for any loss, damage, injury, or inconvenience that may occur to anyone while using this book. You are responsible for your own safety and health while following the walking trips described here. Always check local conditions, know your limitations, and consult a map.

Acknowledgments

I would like to thank Harold McMillan, Sylvia Orozco, and Luann Williams for providing historical background.

Author's Note

It's been a pleasure to put together this selection of rambles and hikes through the parks and streets of Austin, and I hope that you, dear walker, have as much fun doing them as I did writing them. If you complete them all, I guarantee you will know more about the city's nooks and crannies and its history than 90% of your fellow Austinites!

The decor inside Nau's Clarksville drugstore is unchanged since it opened in 1951 (see Walk 10, page 51).

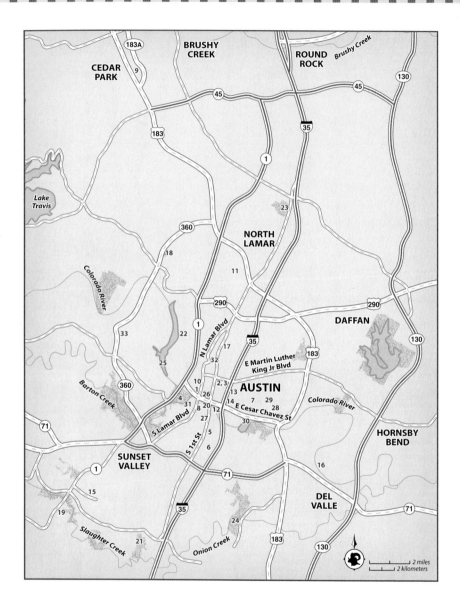

183A

BRUSHY
CREEK

ROUND
ROCK

Brushy Creek

CEDAR
PARK

9

130

45

45

183

35

1

130

Lake
Travis

360

23

NORTH
LAMAR

18

11

Colorado River

290

290

1

DAFFAN

33

22

130

25

17

N Lamar Blvd

35

E Martin Luther
King Jr Blvd

183

32

Barton Creek

360

10

2, 3

AUSTIN

13

7   29

14

28

Colorado River

71

4   31

1   26

8 20

12

27

E Cesar Chavez St

30

S Lamar Blvd

S 1st St

5

HORNSBY
BEND

6

SUNSET
VALLEY

1

71

16

DEL
VALLE

15

71

19

35

24

Slaughter Creek

21

183

Onion Creek

130

2 miles
2 kilometers

Table of Contents

Introduction

Ancient Rome was built on seven hills, while Austin has been shaped and defined by its seven creeks and the Colorado River. Mirabeau Lamar, Texas's first president, chose this spot for the new republic's capital because he was entranced by the beauty of the wooded streams and bluffs he discovered here. The boundaries of the original city were the river and the newly christened Shoal and Waller Creeks, and Barton Creek has always been the jewel in the city's violet crown, a spring-fed symbol of the quality of life in a city that has long topped "best places to live" lists. As the city has grown, it has had to grapple with flood-prone watercourses that have many times washed away dams and houses and people. The Lower Colorado River Authority (LCRA) tamed the Colorado in the 1930s and '40s with the construction of the Highland Lakes, and the city has become much better at managing

An overwater section of the Lady Bird Lake Boardwalks (see Walk 20, page 110)

Austin's watersheds, with exciting plans under way for both Waller and Shoal Creeks that aim to integrate the delicate beauty of the natural environment into daily urban life. One hopes that Lamar would approve.

These walks aim to offer a little more than a guided stroll through pleasant surroundings, though of course we hope that they do meet that basic requirement. We will look for clues and portals to this ambitious city's ever-disappearing past among the skyscrapers and malls. It demonstrates some measure of human progress that only 200 years ago this was a tiny settlement on the banks of a wild river way out on the far-flung frontier, where a few farmers lived under the constant threat of attack from the Mexican army or Indian natives. President Lamar sent Judge Edwin Waller to oversee the design and construction of his new capital, and we will explore the original 640-acre grid conceived by the judge. We will visit the city's first expansion west across Shoal Creek, as well as the first northern and southern suburbs. We will wander through the city's more recent musical history and learn something about the influence and experiences of the Mexican American and African American populations. In addition, many of these walks explore the surprisingly wild parklands that surround many of the city's streams. Austin has retained not only much of the natural beauty that attracted Lamar, but also the wilderness the settlers and Indians knew lay hidden in the woods, canyons, and cliffs along these creeks. Along the way you might acquire a little local knowledge—who William Cannon was, for example (page 117), or why Austinites use the phrase "the violet crown" (page 8).

Although this book is intended for pedestrians, many of the walks would work just as well for those on bicycles or scooters, especially since Austin's traffic is always bad and street parking in popular areas is often next to impossible. In the central city, bikes are available for rent from Austin B-cycle, Jump (Uber), and Pace. Bird and Lime rent scooters. Download those apps to get started. A list of bike- and scooter-friendly walks can be found in the Appendix (page 181).

Greenery along Shoal Creek Greenbelt (see Walk 26, page 136)

1 Austin's Mexico
The Forgotten Barrio

BOUNDARIES: Fifth St. between Blanco and Comal Sts.
DISTANCE: 3 miles
DIFFICULTY: Easy
PARKING: On-street parking at Orchard St. and surrounding streets
PUBLIC TRANSIT: Buses 4 and 663 to stop 2106

Goaded by Mexican president Santa Anna's increasingly repressive rule, Texians fought and won the revolution of 1835–1836 and declared themselves a republic, and the riverside trading post of Waterloo was renamed and made the new state's capital. Jobs in the city attracted Latinos from the surrounding ranchlands, and by the mid-1870s some 300 new arrivals were living around Republic Square, then called Hemphill Square. This new Spanish-speaking community called it Guadalupe Park, but Anglos started referring to it as Mexican Park, and the area around it became known as Austin's Mexico. Despite prejudice, a lack of city services, tough working conditions, and bad housing, Mexican American families flourished for 50 years in the area between the river and Fifth Street, and West Avenue and Colorado to the apartment block rising opposite. These families forged a vital strand of the city's DNA. Without Mexican art, food, and hard work, the city that has long been at or near the top of every ranking would be a much less interesting place.

Though the old barrios have long since been replaced by new buildings, this walk invites you to imagine life here in the late 1800s and early 1900s, when you could have smelled the chile factory, seen children on their way to the Our Lady of Guadalupe school, or mingled with the crowds at the Diez y Seis parade. A council resolution from August 2011 designated the route along Fifth Street from Republic Park to Plaza Saltillo as the Mexican American Heritage Corridor, and this is what we will explore. We will also visit three small but fascinating museums at Brush Square. Note that these museums are open Wednesday–Sunday, from noon to 5 p.m.

Walk Description

Start at ❶ Nate's Baked Goods & Coffee, hidden away down Orchard Street in a sweet old white house with a tin roof, where you can find freshly made sandwiches and turmeric lattes. Take your food to the shaded patio and turn your attention to the house next door, 403 Orchard St., a neat white building with blue trim hiding behind a tree. Both the house and Nate's stand in contrast to the vast apartment block rising opposite, where fresh concrete has already buried any trace of the lives lived there. But the little houses on Orchard have done their own forgetting. We know that a family called Quintanilla lived in a casita at #403, but that is about all we know about them.

After finishing your coffee, walk north on Orchard Street and turn right onto Fifth Street. Turn left onto Baylor Street to find ❷ Treaty Oak Park. This tree was 100 years old when Columbus arrived on the continent, and legend has it that Stephen F. Austin signed a treaty with the Tonkawa under its branches. Once part of a grove known as the Council Oaks, it luckily escaped the axe in the 1920s and also survived a mysterious poisoning attempt in 1989.

Return to Fifth Street and continue across North Lamar Boulevard to honor a new Austin tradition: a selfie at the ❸ ATX sign. It's on the northeastern side of this junction at the edge of the Whole Foods Market parking lot. The market commissioned the piece from Greg and Sharon Keshishian of Austin's Ion Art, who are responsible for many of the city's best-known signs. (For more on the history of Whole Foods Market, see "Clarksville," page 51.)

Continue east on the north side of Fifth Street, crossing Bowie Street and pausing over Shoal Creek to acknowledge the western boundary of both "Mexico" and Austin. Take a look up the channel. The creek is surrounded by high-rise apartment buildings, but in the 1870s it passed through a field at the edge of the city, and many of the city's poor lived in shacks along its banks.

Continue across West Avenue and Rio Grande Street, and turn right onto Nueces Street. We are coming into the heart of the old barrio. At the end of the block on the right in a low-slung brick building is ❹ Mellow Johnny's Bike Shop, founded in 2008 by hometown hero–turned– pariah Lance Armstrong. The Juan Pelota coffee shop is a good pitstop for watching the condo dwellers walk their tiny dogs in the shadow of the skyscrapers. The name Mellow Johnny is a play on *maillot jaune,* the race leader's yellow jersey, and Juan Pelota is cod-Spanish for "one ball," a reference to the result of Armstrong's bout with testicular cancer.

Kitty-corner to Juan Pelota is a parking garage. In the early 1900s this was the site of Walker's Austex Chile Co. factory. Originally between Third and Fourth Streets on the west side of Guadalupe Street, at some point in the early 1900s it moved one block west to this location on San Antonio Street. It was one of the most important places in Austin's Mexico, as all Walker's employees except the administrators were Mexican American at a time when many businesses refused to hire Mexicans.

Continue south on Nueces past the 360 condos. Luis' Cantina was the name of the neighborhood bar at the corner of Third Street, where Trifecta is now. South of Third Street, more high-rises are going up along a revitalized Shoal Creek, where there used to be a flour mill and a park.

Walk east along the tree-lined corridor that is Second Street, one of Austin's most stylish thoroughfares. Cross San Antonio Street, and about halfway along the block on the south side was the site of the Austin Tortilla Manufacturing Company, which in 1929 made 3,000 tortillas a day.

On reaching Guadalupe Street, our walk turns back north to the Fifth Street corridor, but let's pause to take in the J. P. Schneider Store on the corner, one of Austin's most historic buildings. Jacob Schneider, whose parents emigrated from Germany to New Braunfels, was a successful entrepreneur; this was his second store, after the business outgrew its first location. It opened in 1873, and people came from as far as New Braunfels, fording the river at Nueces Street to shop and gather in the store's yard, which had space for 50 wagons. It is now ❺ Lambert's Downtown Barbecue, chef Lou Lambert's thriving upscale stab at the central Texas staple.

Walk north. Our next stop is ❻ Republic Square, which covers the block to the north between Fourth and Fifth and Guadalupe and San Antonio. This was Hemphill Square, one of Edwin Waller's four original city squares. The park was a center of "Mexico's" social life. Families gathered under the live oak trees after church to enjoy candy or tamales from itinerant sellers. It was also the scene of the annual Diez y Seis de Septiembre parade, held here until 1927. The event honors Mexico's declaration of independence from Spain. After the 1928 city plan forced the community to move to the south and east side (see "East Austin," page 75, and "Tejano Trails," page 159), the park fell into disuse. Republic Square was renamed and reopened in 1976 in honor of the country's bicentennial and has been transformed into a flourishing urban center. Pick up fresh veggies and treats at the Saturday farmers market. The *Blackbird* sculpture on the north side is by local artist Holly Kincannon and draws inspiration from the city's ubiquitous grackles and from Oaxacan folk art.

To the west is the gleaming new ❼ **Federal Courthouse,** by Mack Scogin Merrill Elam Architects of Atlanta, which opened in 2012 on the site of the infamous Intel shell, an unfinished structure that the chip manufacturer commissioned and then abandoned. Sycamore trees and benches line the pedestrian-only portion of San Antonio Street in front of the courthouse, a pleasant transition from the square to the building's banded limestone exterior.

Experience modern Mexican art and culture at Mexic-Arte Museum.

Our walk now leaves Austin's Mexico, as we continue east past the bars and restaurants that line Fifth Street between Guadalupe Street and Congress Avenue. For now, the tide of construction in the blocks around Congress Avenue has retreated. It left new landmarks like the the Austonian and the Marriott Hotel (built on the site of beloved Mexican restaurant Las Manitas), but older, smaller brick buildings still set the tone along the avenue. One of these is the ❽ **Mexic-Arte Museum,** a white building topped with a Mexican-looking frieze at the junction of Fifth Street. The gallery features modern Mexican art, and you will find work from contemporary Latino artists, as well as a gift store full of Mexican-style gifts. Director Sylvia Orozco worked with the city to develop the Mexican American History Corridor that we are following.

Come back onto Congress Avenue and turn right onto Fifth Street, continuing past the murals on the long north side of the Mexic-Arte. The building across the alley with the handsome arched entrances is the Phillips Building, a last outpost of Austin's Mexico. In the 1920s it was a Studebaker dealership, but in the 1940s it was a dance hall that was popular with the Mexican American community.

Continue east three blocks to arrive at the northwest corner of Brush Square, another of the four original city parks. Admire Austin Central Fire Station 1, a lovely Art Deco structure from the 1930s. The extension at the eastern end of the building, added in the 1960s, houses the **❾ Austin Fire Museum**. Next door are two older houses, moved here from other locations to form a fascinating historical triptych. The fire museum has an engrossing display of equipment and riveting photographs, including communication equipment from the 1960s and a section honoring the department's African American firefighters.

The house next door, the **❿ O. Henry Museum**, was built in the 1880s and moved to this location in the 1930s. It was opened as a museum in 1934. The writer himself rented the house for only a couple of years in the 1890s, long before he became O. Henry. As William Sidney Porter, he lived there with his wife, Athol, and daughter, Margaret, before moving to Houston to take a position with the *Houston Post*. He had worked at the First National Bank of Austin before moving to Houston, and his burgeoning career in the bigger city was cut short when an audit of the bank's books led to embezzlement charges and he went to prison in Ohio. He began writing short stories during his time in jail, and it was there that he took on his famous pseudonym. Though he did not invent the sobriquet, his use of the phrase "city of the violet crown" to describe Austin (in a piece titled "Tictocq: The Great French Detective") solidified it into local parlance.

How can you say you've been to Austin if you don't have a selfie from the ATX sign at Whole Foods Market?

The last building on this side of the square is the ⓫ Joseph and Susanna Dickinson Hannig Museum, which displays artifacts from and information about the eventful life of Susanna. She was the "Messenger of the Alamo," chosen by General Santa Anna to take the news of his victory to Sam Houston. This house was built in the German style by Joseph, her fifth husband, a handsome cabinetmaker who was 20 years her junior and who had been a frequent guest at her boardinghouse in Lockhart.

The last two stops on this walk are a work in progress, and because they are across the highway and several blocks away from each other, you might want to end here. I suggest finding a rental scooter or bike to complete the tour.

Leaving the Dickinson Museum, go south on Neches Street, along the eastern side of Brush Square. At Fourth Street, cross the street and turn left, walking by the bike lane past the Convention Center and the Hilton and then crossing Waller Creek by Palm Park. Take care crossing the frontage roads at I-35 as there are no pedestrian lights. Welcome to East Austin! You have just put into practice the idea behind the Mexican American History Corridor, which is to connect the fading stories of Austin's Mexico to the ongoing history of Mexican East Austin. (See "Tejano Trails," page 159, for more on this area.) Following Fourth Street east, turn left at Waller Street, cross the railroad tracks, and come to Fifth Street. The city intends for the patch of green to your left to be a plaza with a rain garden and public art, though there are issues with construction costs and right-of-way.

Walk north up Waller to East Sixth Street, and turn right then left on Attayac Street. Cross Seventh to Lydia Street, kitty-corner from Attayac. Our next stop, ⓬ Our Lady of Guadalupe Church, is two blocks north, at Lydia and Ninth Street. Ministering primarily to the Mexican American community, the church was founded at Fifth and Guadalupe, by Republic Square in the old barrio, in 1916, the year that Austin's school board decided to send non-English-speaking children to different schools. The congregation moved here in 1926. This handsome building, with space for 700, features tall columns and a high white cupola and dates from 1953.

Turn right onto Ninth Street, passing the southern side of the church, to Navasota Street. Cross the street and turn right, passing the Texas State Cemetery. Cross East Seventh and Sixth Streets, coming back to East Fifth. Turn left, and after a block you will arrive at ⓭ Plaza Saltillo, built in 1998 with the assistance of Austin's sister city of Saltillo, which donated the benches. The open breezeways and shades of faded pink are a reminder of the colors of that city's famous tile.

The southbound train on the 550 MetroRail Red Line leaves every hour or so from Plaza Saltillo and will take you one stop to the Convention Center at Fourth Street and Neches, from which you can find your way back to your car.

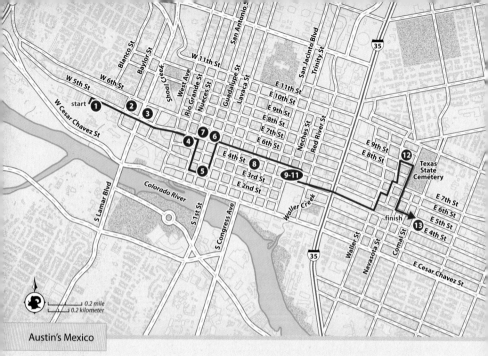

Points of Interest

1 Nate's Baked Goods & Coffee 401 Orchard St., 512-350-2084, natesbakedaustin.com

2 Treaty Oak Park 507 Baylor St.

3 ATX sign Fifth St. and N. Lamar Blvd.

4 Mellow Johnny's Bike Shop 400 Nueces St., 512-473-0222, mellowjohnnys.com

5 Lambert's Downtown Barbecue 401 W. Second St., 512-494-1500, lambertsaustin.com

6 Republic Square 422 Guadalupe St.

7 Federal Courthouse Plaza Fifth St. and San Antonio St.

8 Mexic-Arte Museum 419 Congress Ave., 512-480-9373, mexic-artemuseum.org

9 Austin Fire Museum 401 E. Fifth St., 512-974-3835, austinfiremuseum.org

10 O. Henry Museum 409 E. Fifth St., 512-974-1398, austintexas.gov/department/o-henry-museum

11 Joseph and Susanna Dickinson Hannig Museum 411 E. Fifth St., 512-974-3830, austintexas.gov/department/joseph-and-susanna-dickinson-hannig-museum

12 Our Lady of Guadalupe Church 1206 E. Ninth St., 512-537-3641, olgaustin.org

13 Plaza Saltillo E. Fifth St. and Comal St.

2 Austin's Music Landmarks, Part 1
Looking for Lost Chords

Above: Colombian American singer Kali Uchis wows a sold-out Stubb's.

BOUNDARIES: E. 17th St., Guadalupe St., Red River St., E. Second St.
DISTANCE: 2 miles
DIFFICULTY: Easy
PARKING: Paid on-street parking around E. 10th St.
PUBLIC TRANSIT: Buses 6, 7, 10, 103, 111, 142, 171, and 935 to stop 864

Austin was a music town even before the dazed days of the Armadillo, but the hippie cowboy days of the 1970s are the city's acknowledged golden era. It was a sleepy college town where the longhairs and the rednecks and the politicians pretty much kept to themselves, until Eddie Wilson opened the Armadillo. Willie Nelson came back from Nashville, and all the guys dug his music and dug being around the pretty girls, and everybody got along. Thus was born the Cosmic Cowboy era, and guitar-slingers and songwriters moved to town from all over to live in cheap apartments and play for tips. The city engaged warp drive in 1994 when Johnny Cash played South by Southwest and the conference inaugurated the Interactive Festival. Band manager Roland Swenson had traveled to New York in the mid-'80s for the New Music Seminar and returned with an idea, and his cool little event became the mega-festival that draws thousands of people to Austin every March from all over the world. Austin began calling itself the "Live Music Capital of the World," and justifiably. The music scene has remained vital, with local artists like current darlings Sweet Spirit and Molly Burch getting airplay and attention, and a constant parade of touring acts passing through town to play at Moody Theatre or the Circuit of the Americas. This walk is designed to take you back through Austin's history of riffage to look at some landmarks where you still might hear the ghostly echoes of a killer solo from 40 years ago. Some have disappeared, but most are still going strong.

We have divided this walk into two sections, north and south of the Colorado River. Part 1 winds roughly southwest from East 10th and Red River to East Second and Lavaca. Part 2 is listed separately (page 18). Both sections might benefit from the use of a rented scooter or bike.

Walk Description

Let's begin at a place with some real history! Austin's oldest music venue, located just north of the Capitol on San Jacinto Boulevard, predates Willie Nelson and the Armadillo by more than a century. Opened in 1866 by August Scholz, ❶ Scholz Garten is the longest continuously operated business west of the Mississippi. This convivial beer joint and restaurant has long been a been a favorite of UT football fans and Texas politicians. Head out back to the garden area for Texas tunes and fare and German beer. Perhaps the first celebrity to enjoy the Scholz vibe was General Custer, who hung out here when his cavalry was stationed in Austin. A few years later William Porter (better known as the writer O. Henry) was a regular with his group the Hill City Quartette.

From Scholz Garten walk south on San Jacinto Boulevard, crossing 15th Street and passing the eastern side of the Capitol grounds. Turn left at East 10th Street, and go three blocks to Red River Street. This street has become Austin's punk Music Row, with clubs like Beerland and Cheer Up Charlie's serving up raucous live music. On the corner of 10th and Red River you will find the daddy of the scene, now more than 10 years old. This is the 900-person-capacity ❷ Mohawk, the best place in Austin to hear the grungier end of rock music. A multilevel deck and mezzanine offer great views of the outside stage, which has become a place to see edgier established acts such as recent visitors Thurston Moore, Liz Phair, and John Lydon's PIL.

Cross Red River and walk two blocks south to what is now ❸ Stubb's Bar-B-Q at Eighth and Red River. This building by Waller Creek has been pivotal in the Austin music scene since the 1970s, when it was a dive bar called the ❹ One Knite. This was where the kids who were hooked on the blues played for tips to an audience that included biker gangs, local legends like the Guacamole Queen (as mentioned by Frank Zappa on *One Size Fits All*), and even, apparently, Lyndon Johnson's Secret Service detail. Jimmie Vaughan, Stevie Ray Vaughan, Paul Ray, and others were defining a certain Austin sound—a rocking but funky and very stoned version of the blues they copied from East Austin musicians like T. D. Bell and Erbie Bowser, who played black clubs like the Victory Grill, the Hi-El Club, and Charlie's. The police tried to shut the bar down; at one point they raided it 120 times in three months. But it was the IRS whose demands eventually closed the place, ironically after an impossibly crowded Willie Nelson show.

Joe Ely was a regular at the One Knite. He and the Flatlanders dragged their dusty sound from Lubbock to the capital after the Hub City gang had honed their chops at jam sessions at Stubb's, just east of Lubbock's I-27. The amiable owner, Christopher B. Stubblefield, became a mentor to the young musicians. In the mid-1980s the IRS got his restaurant too, so Stubb demolished it with a bulldozer and moved to Austin, where he started another restaurant that sadly did not last long. He suffered a heart attack in 1989, and friends, including Ely's wife, Sharon, rallied around and helped him start a sauce business, which became successful enough that the investors began looking at funding a new Stubb's restaurant. Though Stubb died in 1995 of heart failure, both the sauce business and the restaurant became separately successful. Charles Attal, the Austin promoter who is now part of the C3 group that puts on the Austin City Limits Music Festival, took over the restaurant and built a venue in time for South by Southwest 1996, at which the Fugees performed on the outdoor stage in the rain. By next year the roof was in place, and the venue was established as one of the best in Austin for touring acts.

Our next stop is at East Sixth and Red River. This is the site of the original Austin ❺ Emo's, which is still operating south of the river on East Riverside Avenue. By the '90s, punk and grunge had kicked blues and country to the sidelines for a spell, and this location of Emo's was the dirty mainline for the hard-edged music of those times. Punk to the core; all-ages; and, for a few years at least, without a cover, it was where the misfits and metal kids went for loud sounds and cheap beer. Local bands like Ed Hall, Steel Pole Bath Tub, Squat Thrust, and Noodle packed the place with their circus grunge metal. It was on this club's outdoor stage that Johnny Cash (and the Tennessee Three) and Beck performed at the 1994 South by Southwest.

From here, go west along the strip of bars known as Dirty Sixth to The Rooftop on Sixth at 403 E. Sixth St. A more traditional strain of rock and roll flourished here in the '90s at a club called the ❻ Steamboat. Here patrons drank and danced to a funkier, bluesier sound more directly related to the old Austin sound of the '70s—after all, Stevie Ray Vaughan played here—but raucous, rocking, and ready to party. Danny Crooks, the manager, nurtured a local scene that included Joe Rockhead, the Scabs, Sister 7, and Ian Moore. The building is one of the classic old Victorian storefronts on Sixth Street.

A block west at 313 E. Sixth St. is the Midnight Cowboy Lounge, a cocktail bar named after the Asian massage business that occupied the premises for ages. It was also the site of the ❼ **Black Cat Lounge.** In the early '90s, Soulhat (grunge jam-band hippies) and Two Hoots and a Holler (blasting roots music) held sway here under the baleful and erratic eye of owner Paul Sessums, who cursed the band out if they played for less than 3 hours at a stretch. You could grab a free hot dog—Sessums gave them away after the health department told him he could not sell them—buy a can of Pabst Blue Ribbon, and chill to the music on the bleacher seats until 2 a.m. Sessums feuded incessantly with the city and the community association and eventually left the management of the club to his daughter. He died in a van wreck in 1998, but the venue kept going until it was destroyed by fire in July 2002.

Continue west along East Sixth Street and turn left on San Jacinto Boulevard, passing the Westin. Cross East Fifth Street and turn left. The familiar logo shines over the new location of

❽ **Antone's Nightclub,** not far from its original location at Sixth and Brazos opposite the Driskill Hotel. Port Arthur native Clifford Antone opened the "home of the blues" in 1975, making a splash with a weekend residency from Clifton Chenier. The list of legends that played at the venue is staggering: Muddy Waters, Jimmy Reed, Willie Dixon, John Lee Hooker, Fats Domino, Buddy Guy, and B. B. King, to name a few. The club moved from Sixth Street to North Austin and then came back to the UT area on Guadalupe Street for the '80s and most of the '90s, its longest and most successful run. Acts like the Fabulous Thunderbirds and Doug Sahm tore the place up night after night. Antone was forced to give up the club after a 2000 conviction for dealing marijuana, and he died in 2006, a few years after his release. But his legacy is intact. His sister

Hurray for the Riff Raff play on the outdoor stage at Mohawk

Susan Antone now runs the club, where old favorites like Maceo Parker, Guy Forsyth, and Miss Lavelle White keep the blues alive.

Turn around and walk along East Fifth Street to Congress Avenue, two blocks west. Turn left on Congress, and pause at the end of the block in front of the soaring Frost Bank Tower. This used to be ❾ **Club Foot**, where the '80s hit Austin. The venue was located in a partially underground warehouse next to the Greyhound station, with a large window looking out over the station and a bar made from half a Lincoln Continental. The opening night featured the Stranglers, and U2 played there on their first US tour. R.E.M, the Stray Cats, and Echo and the Bunnymen all passed through. In 1983 it was the site of the first of the *Austin Chronicle* Readers Poll Music Awards, an event that now kicks off South by Southwest.

Cross Congress Avenue at Fourth Street, and look for the Patagonia store in the next block. In 2008 the company moved into the Victorian building that in the late '70s was the home of the ❿ **Vulcan Gas Company.** Psychedelic music struggled to find a home in Austin, as folkies and frat boys disliked the music, and any club that booked the hippie bands was raided by the Liquor Control Board (LCB). A group called the Electric Grandmothers began to produce shows at the Doris Miller Auditorium. They changed their name to the Vulcan Gas Company and opened the club on Congress Avenue. Weary of the LCB, they decided not to sell alcohol and recruited artists like Gilbert Shelton and Jim Franklin to design posters to promote the shows. That art is now worth a great deal of money. Local bands like Conqueroo and the 13th Floor Elevators and national acts like the Velvet Underground played to audiences arranged on church pews. Financial problems and continual harassment by authorities led to the club's closing in the mid-1970s.

Keep south on Congress Avenue and turn right onto West Second Street, which has bloomed into one of the city's most attractive and popular thoroughfares. Walk two blocks to the northwest corner of Lavaca and Second, home of the ⑪ **ACL Live at The Moody Theater** and ⑫ **Willie Nelson statue.** The bronze statue, by Pennsylvania artist Clete Shields, was installed in 2012 on the street that had born the singer's name since 2010, when the city responded to the excitement around the new theater by designating this stretch of West Second Street as Willie Nelson Boulevard. Fittingly, Willie sits at the bottom of the stairs leading to what was immediately recognized as Austin's best music venue. The Moody is a state-of-the-art facility with a capacity of 2,700, and the first-class sound system and great sight lines ensure that there isn't a bad seat in the house. Since it opened in 2011, the venue has presented a stellar list of acts from every musical genre, from Diana Ross to the Arctic Monkeys. Performances for *Austin City Limits* are recorded here, and you can visit acltv.com to register for your chance to win a pass to a taping, or you can join one of the tours that start at 11 a.m. every weekday.

Lambert's Restaurant, in the Schneider building (see "Austin's Mexico," page 4) is next door to the site of ⑬ Liberty Lunch, the long-lost venue that saw its heyday in the '90s. Texas Lighthouse for the Blind served lunches there after World War II, and Austin comedy duo Shannon Sedwick and Michael Shelton (who went on to found Esther's Follies) opened it as a performance space and restaurant in 1975. Legend has it that they found the words LIBERTY LUNCH painted on an old board, which served as a sign for the new venue. The place started to take off when doorman Mark Pratz and his partner J-Net Ward took over in 1983. Together with South by Southwest cofounder Louis Meyers, they began to book reggae and funk bands from New Orleans and Jamaica and then local rap-funk acts like Bad Mutha Goose and Retarted Elf. They kept the venue going until 1999. The long black room with its island mural saw an unmatched list of incredible shows, including Nirvana's last Austin performance on October 21, 1991, and a Sonic Youth show from 1988 that became a famous bootleg. Local musician Michael Hall realized one of the most storied nights in Austin's music history here, the 24 hours of "Gloria" event, which was exactly that. Van Morrison himself was roped in: Hall reached him by phone at a bar in the UK and held the phone up to a microphone as Van the Man sang the famous chorus.

We have reached our last stop north of the river, so this is your chance to bow out for today, if you wish. Otherwise let's continue with Part 2: Walk south on Guadalupe, past City Hall, and over West Cesar Chavez Street. Cross South First Street at the north end of the bridge, and find the pedestrian walkway on its western side, by which you will cross the river.

Bobby Bare Jr. rocks out at Stubb's.

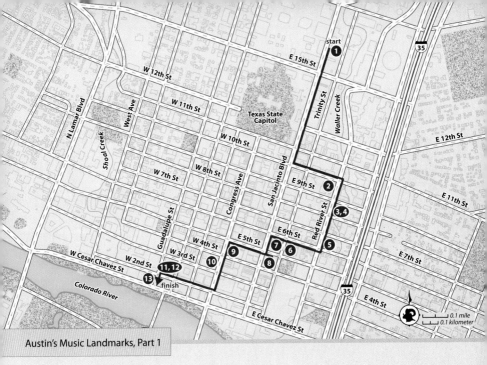

Points of Interest

1 Scholz Garten   1607 San Jacinto Blvd., 512-474-1958, scholzgarten.com

2 Mohawk   912 Red River St., 512-666-0877, mohawkaustin.com

3 Stubb's Bar-B-Q   801 Red River St., 512-480-8341, stubbsaustin.com

4 Former site of One Knite   801 Red River St.

5 Former site of Emo's   600 E. Sixth St.

6 Former site of Steamboat   403 E. Sixth St.

7 Former site of Black Cat Lounge   313 E. Sixth St.

8 Antone's Nightclub   305 E. Fifth St., 512-814-0361, antonesnightclub.com

9 Former site of Club Foot   110 E. Fourth St.

10 Former site of Vulcan Gas Company   316 Congress Ave.

11 ACL Live at The Moody Theater   310 W. Willie Nelson Blvd., 512-225-7999, acl-live.com

12 Willie Nelson statue   310 W. Willie Nelson Blvd.

13 Former site of Liberty Lunch   405 W. Second St.

3 Austin's Music Landmarks, Part 2
Looking for Lost Chords

Above: *C-Boy's Heart & Soul is waiting for you.*

BOUNDARIES: Colorado River, Bouldin Ave., S. Congress Ave., Leland St.
DISTANCE: 1.6 miles
DIFFICULTY: Easy
PARKING: Paid parking at Vic Mathias Shores or at the Long Center
PUBLIC TRANSIT: Buses 1, 7, 20, and 801 to stop 2767

This is the second part of this walk, taking in some musical landmarks on the south side of the river. Read the introduction to Part 1 (page 11) for more background information.

Walk Description

Start at the lakeshore at Vic Mathias Shores, just west of the South First Street bridge, where you'll find a gazebo, a pond, and some exercise machines along the Ann and Roy Butler Hike and Bike

Trail. The trailhead deck here was renamed ❶ **Brent Grulke Plaza** in honor of the former director of South by Southwest. Nebraska native Grulke was a key player in the Austin music scene from the '80s on, gaining experience and contacts from his years as a road manager and sound engineer. He stepped in to direct the South by Southwest Music Festival when Louis Meyers left in 1994 and stayed in the job until his untimely death in 2012. Grulke was as important to South by Southwest as the festival is to the city. His was the steady hand on the wheel as the event grew from its indie roots into the all-consuming monster it is today. He knew exactly how to give the record companies what they wanted and still maintain enough artistic control to keep the event compelling for the fans and journalists. This plaza celebrates a man who stayed true to himself and his friends, who was truly passionate about music, and who never stopped trying to help those who wanted to succeed.

A short walk west will bring you to the ❷ **statue of Stevie Ray Vaughan**, who stands with his back to Lady Bird Lake with his trademark cloak, hat, and Stratocaster. Born in Dallas, Vaughan picked up the guitar at the age of 10, inspired by older brother Jimmie, and learned to play the blues by ear. Soon he was playing at clubs around the Metroplex. He dropped out of school, moved to Austin, and began building a reputation that resulted in the "Let's Dance" gig with David Bowie, which propelled him to international stardom. Vaughan died in a helicopter accident on a foggy Wisconsin night in 1990, just as he was recovering from a career dip. His incandescent talent can be seen on many videos on YouTube, but sadly nothing from the glorious nights in the early '70s at the One Knite was recorded, and those legendary times are only a fading memory for an older generation. This statue, by Ralph Helmick, was placed here in 1994 and, like Willie's (page 15), has become a place for fans to pay their respects.

Leave Stevie Ray and walk away from the river to Riverside Drive. Turn left on this busy street, and cross South First and then Barton Springs Road. Cross Riverside and come to the site of Threadgill's World Headquarters. This recently closed and much-missed restaurant, a spin-off from the original Threadgill's location on North Lamar Boulevard (see "Crestview," page 59), is next to the site of the venue for which the city is most famous, the ❸ **Armadillo World Headquarters**. Austinite Eddie Wilson found the place, which had been a National Guard Armory, in 1970, and a gang of hippies turned the shell into the coolest beer garden and concert venue ever. Shiva's Headband, a local band that Wilson managed, played the opening show in 1970. The venue's tolerant atmosphere brought acts to Texas that would otherwise have left the state off their itineraries, and on August 12, 1972, Willie Nelson walked onto the stage and changed Austin music forever. According to a 2017 interview Wilson did for *Austin Monthly*, "it was girls in halter-tops. That's what caused the petri dish to runneth over. When the rednecks were coming into the beer garden and seeing the hippie girls in their bell-bottoms, they'd immediately start missing haircuts. And the hippies were already wearing cowboy hats, because if they wanted to buy a case of beer when they were traveling, they had to put their hair out of sight. The costumes were interchangeable, and the hormones were raging." Things ratcheted up later that year when the Dead came to town. "Jerry Garcia played Thanksgiving Day of '72. Nobody knew it was going to happen. It's what I called the inoculation of the Armadillo. From there on, things didn't have to make sense." AC/DC played their first American gig here in 1976, and the venue embraced punk rock too, with shows from the Ramones, the Talking Heads, and the Clash, who made their "Rock the Casbah" video in Austin. Wilson opened Threadgill's World Headquarters in 1996 as a shrine to the glory days of the '70s, and it famously features the Southern cuisine that Wilson served at the Armadillo. The old Austin spirit comes alive on Sunday morning at the regular Gospel Brunch.

The last four places we will visit are all along South Congress Avenue, which is known for its bohemian stores and range of restaurants. This wide thoroughfare with the great view of the Capitol is both on the must-visit list for tourists and a popular hangout for locals. It is covered in this book, so if you wish to dawdle, take a look at that entry (page 141). Our last location is a mile up the hill from Threadgill's, so you might consider hopping on a scooter for this section.

Go east along Riverside Drive, and then turn right (south) South Congress Avenue, passing the Texas School for the Deaf. At the first traffic light, cross to the junction of South Congress and Academy Drive, which is currently a building site. This was the third and final location of ❹ Soap Creek Saloon, which closed for good in 1985. According the Eddie Wilson, the original location at the top of a hill off Bee Cave Road in now tony West Lake Hills was just as responsible as the Armadillo for the redneck/hippie cocktail that defined Austin culture for decades. Doug Sahm, who was the living embodiment of this mixture even though he was from San Antonio, was a frequent performer and rented a house close by. Sahm and Freddy Fender were the most famous members of the Soap Creek family, playing their country psychedelia for the marijuana- and tequila-laced, cowboy-hat-wearing longhairs. The club moved up to North Austin for a while before coming to South Congress Avenue, where it joined the Continental Club and the Austex Lounge to form what Austin writer and scene den mother Margaret Moser called the South Austin Triple Crown.

Continue east along Academy Drive past Hotel Saint Cecilia. Turn left into a large parking lot. At the back of the lot, there is a low white building that was the ❺ Austin Opera House. Willie Nelson owned it and opened the venue on June 28, 1977, with a week of shows. His partner Tim O'Connor (of the Backyard and Austin Music Hall) took it over. It closed in 1990 but reopened as the Terrace for a few years. The building now houses a software company and, more relevantly, the famous Arlyn Studios, owned by Willie's nephew Freddy Fletcher and his wife and business partners. Everyone from Childish Gambino to David Crosby has recorded here.

Walk back to Congress Avenue and go south on the east side of the street to come to ❻ The Continental Club, the city's most famous music bar and the place where the Austin sound lives on. Frequented by tourists and locals alike, the Continental has risen to the rank of unofficial national treasure under the careful stewardship of Steve Wertheimer, who took over the club in 1987. He took a chance and booked a country picker called Junior Brown. Word got out about this guit-steel-slinging straight arrow in a cowboy hat, and the venue took off. Wertheimer had taken over the club from Mark Pratz and J-Net Ward when they opened the Lunch (page 16). Back in the '80s the club played host to local rock acts like the True Believers, the Leroi Brothers, and Poi Dog Pondering. The business originally opened in 1947 as a laundromat, and became a private jazz club in 1955. It floundered through the '60s as a dive bar and disco but began to flourish again when the former One Knite (page 13) owners took it over in 1979. Apart from Scholz's (page 12), The Continental Club is the only venue in the city that has stayed open in the same location with the same name for its entire history.

Our last stop is ❼ C-Boy's Heart & Soul. Also run by Wertheimer, it bills itself as "the swankiest club on South Congress," and I would not argue. Named for C-Boy Parks, the much-loved owner of long-defunct West Campus bar the Rome Inn, the club serves adult drinks in a grown-up atmosphere along with some serious blues, R&B, and jazz. Wertheimer has transformed the place that used to be Trophy's, South Congress' last true dive bar, into his upscale take on a classic neighborhood juke joint. Don't miss the Jade Room lounge upstairs, which is modeled after a '50s Japanese GI bar. To get a taste of the room's ambience, listen to the Jimmie Vaughan Trio's *Live at C-Boys* album, which was recorded here in 2017. Vaughan and his brother Stevie Ray were regular attractions at the Rome Inn, and at C-Boy's he keeps the tradition. Accompanied by organist Mike Flanigin, he holds court on the small stage every other weekend at 10:30 p.m. If you time it right, seeing this Austin legend play would be a fitting end to this deep dive back into the history of Austin's music.

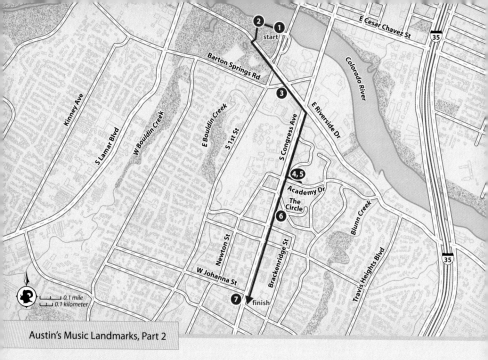

Points of Interest

1 Brent Grulke Plaza Auditorium Shores

2 Statue of Stevie Ray Vaughan Auditorium Shores

3 Armadillo World Headquarters 301 W. Riverside Dr., 512-472-9304, threadgills.com

4 Former site of Soap Creek Saloon South Congress Ave. and Academy Dr.

5 Former site of Austin Opera House 200 Academy Dr.

6 The Continental Club 1315 S. Congress Ave., 512-441-2444, continentalclub.com

7 C-Boy's Heart & Soul 2008 S. Congress Ave., 512-215-0023, cboys.com

4 Barton Creek Greenbelt
Uncle Billy's Creek

Above: *The Flats on Barton Creek after a rainstorm*

BOUNDARIES: Barton Springs Road, Barton Hills Dr., Mopac Expy. (TX 1), Loop 360
DISTANCE: 4.4 miles
DIFFICULTY: Moderate
PARKING: At Zilker Park
PUBLIC TRANSIT: Bus 30 to stop 4081

Hiking the Greenbelt is one of the quintessential Austin experiences, coming close behind swimming in Barton Springs itself, eating a breakfast taco, or being stuck in traffic. This park covers nearly 2,000 acres of dense greenery and steep bluffs on either side of the city's iconic Barton Creek, the most famous of the creeks and streams that burst from the limestone caves and crannies of the Edwards Plateau. For many years the springs and Zilker Park were the only publicly accessible areas, and people would climb or crawl under fences to get to the swimming pools and cliffs farther upstream. During the 1990s, the Trust for Public Land started acquiring land along the creek and donating it to the city, and the greenbelt expanded by more than 1,000 acres in that decade. That process continues, and in the 2000s the Hill Country Conservancy began to realize their vision of a regional trail system that would connect Austin with Hays County to the south. They have spruced up and rebranded the route as the Violet Crown Trail, a nod to Austin's nickname, The City of the Violet Crown. This newish route splits from the Greenbelt trail west of Loop 360 and reaches a new trailhead on US 290 at Sunset Valley, and hikers now have roughly 10 miles of trails to explore in total. The most noticeable signs of this renovation are the marker posts that appear every 0.25 mile and at trail junctions. Surprisingly the Greenbelt is not nearly the biggest urban park in the United States, but it's one of the best and is practically synonymous with outdoor recreation in Austin. From the first steps it can be hard to remember that you are only minutes from downtown. In fact it has only been since 2003, when the Frost Bank building was finished, that you could see downtown from the Barton Springs pool.

Walk Description

For an out-and-back walk, we will explore the first 2 miles of the trail from ❶ Zilker Metropolitan Park to Gus Fruh Pool. And as mentioned, weather and water permitting, there are opportunities to swim and climb along the way, and naturally you could take your bike. There are no restrooms or other amenities on the trail, so be prepared, carry water, and take your trash home, including puppy poop, which pollutes the stream where people and fish swim.

From the Zilker trailhead, head upstream on a wide, level path through a grassy meadow to reach the shade of the riparian forest of cottonwoods and hackberry. The gravel surface gives way to the familiar Hill Country rocks and roots. Look for flowering plants like yellow goldeneye in sunny spots, and ferns and cattails in wet areas. As for fauna, raccoons and foxes live here, as do rattlesnakes, so be mindful on the more remote parts of the trail.

About 0.8 mile from the trailhead, there is a dogleg in the river, and the resulting pool is

A climber tackles a wall along Barton Creek.

Backstory: Barton Creek and Springs

Barton Creek and Springs have been a gathering place for people (and animals) for thousands of years. They are named for William Barton, an early settler. He was apparently quite a character, known as the Daniel Boone of Texas. Born in Kentucky, Barton moved to Alabama, where his first wife died. He came to Texas in 1828 with two brothers and was granted land (from the Mexican government) in present-day Bastrop County. But when, in 1837, someone settled within 10 miles of his home, he decamped with his new wife and settled on a bluff above Barton Creek, where his nearest neighbor, Reuben Hornsby of Hornsby Bend, was 11 miles away. It turned out not to be a good move for a loner: his newfound peace was shattered when President Lamar chose Austin as the new capital, ironically because of the plentiful water available from Barton's three springs, which Barton had named Parthenia, Eliza, and Zenobia after his daughters. The property passed through a few owners after old Uncle Billy died, and eventually Andrew Jackson Zilker bought it 1901. Zilker left the springs and the acres that are now Zilker Park to the city, and in 1922 the city got around to constructing a dam and ❷ Barton Springs Pool. The main spring, Parthenia, is under the diving board; Eliza flows into a newly constructed channel on the west side of the pool; and you can venture up the creek's eastern bank to find Zenobia, now called Upper Spring. Although development is an ever-present threat to the water quality, these springs are still flowing, and from way before dawn to long after dusk, you can find Austinites enjoying this sacred place.

a popular swimming spot known as Campbell's Hole. The route splits here for 100 yards or so. Take the left path to explore an area of limestone outcrop called The Flats, often draped with sunbathers and sometimes a raging torrent. The two routes soon come back together, and quite soon you pass the Spyglass access trail. After you cross a drainage that is Skunk Hollow Creek, you will arrive at a small wooden fence and marker post. At this point the main trail crosses the creekbed and continues along the east bank. Stay right. You will pass tall bluffs that attract Austin's climbers, who test themselves on routes with names like Maggie's Wall and Kingdom of Ging.

Forge onward over rougher territory to Gus Fruh Pool, a swimming hole just over 2 miles from the start. Keep an eye out for water moccasins. This is the turnaround point, although the trail continues for many more miles. The Greenbelt branch goes past three falls to end close to the Bluffs of Lost Creek neighborhood off Loop 360. (Study the map at the trailhead or go to violetcrowntrail .com/explore.) But this hike has shown you some of the best the park has to offer, all within a couple of miles of downtown. That's Austin's attraction in a nutshell, and the combination of natural beauty and first-class amenities is what impelled the city's creation and its nearly 200 years of growth and success. With that thought, walk back and head to Barton Springs Pool for a dip.

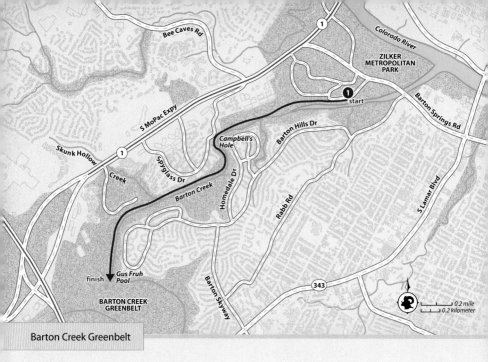

Barton Creek Greenbelt

Points of Interest

1 Zilker Metropolitan Park 2100 Barton Springs Road, austintexas.gov/department /zilker-metropolitan-park

2 Barton Springs Pool 2131 William Barton Dr., 512-974-6300, austintexas.gov/department /barton-springs-pool

5 Blunn Creek Greenbelt
The Heart of Travis Heights

Above: *Nature awaits at Blunn Creek Greenbelt.*

BOUNDARIES: E. Live Oak St., East Side Dr., Alameda Dr.
DISTANCE: 1.4 miles
DIFFICULTY: Easy
PARKING: Street parking at Big Stacy Park or in Travis Heights
PUBLIC TRANSIT: Bus 1 to stop 574

This walk explores the Blunn Creek Greenbelt from Big Stacy Park to Little Stacy Park in historic Travis Heights, South Austin's first suburb. When the Congress Avenue bridge opened in 1887, John Milton Swisher, a financier and public servant, subdivided more than 20 acres of the family farm on either side of what was then the San Antonio road. He gave the streets the names of his family members and was farsighted and generous enough to allow 120 feet for the right-of-way through the subdivision, giving South Congress Avenue the grand view and boulevard style it has today. Swisher sold the north section of the farm to Charles Newning, who built what was called Fairview Park. Newning aimed to sell large houses on leafy creekside lots with views of the city to prosperous Austinites, laying out a rather modern sort of subdivision with winding roads and irregular lot sizes, designed to make best use of the topography. But his dream was thwarted by another very modern problem: the traffic over the bridge became so bad that his intended clientele did not care for the trouble of a river crossing on their way home. Undeterred, Newning's partner General William Harwood Stacy began development of Travis Heights in 1913. (The new Congress Avenue bridge had opened in 1910, ameliorating the traffic problem.) This new suburb promised houses for all income levels set in a mixture of straight and curved streets. Stacy put in deed restrictions against commercial development and ran streetcar service to the neighborhood from the Capitol. The development was heavily promoted and very successful, promising a life "Out of the Noise-Zone and Into the Ozone." Stacy dedicated the land along the creek as a park, and it is thanks to his foresight that Travis Heights remains such a desirable neighborhood, in no small part due to the attractive strip of nature in its center.

Walk Description

Begin in the ❶ Big Stacy Park parking lot at the northeast corner of East Side Drive and Live Oak Street. This lot is mainly used by people visiting Big Stacy pool, located behind a tall fence in front of you. The park was added in the 1930s, a few years after Little Stacy Park, at the other end of the greenbelt. The trail, a concrete path, begins at the northern end of the parking lot, immediately dodges left across Blunn Creek, and then stays on the western bank for the whole walk. Sometimes the route diverges, but you would have to try hard to get lost; keep in the narrow parkland between the creek and East Side Drive.

Continue through a small wood and into a more open area popular with dogs and their owners. The creek and its bank are behind a chain fence designed to protect this strip of nature, though there are two paths that provide access to Travis Heights Elementary, and from them you can take a closer look at the steep limestone banks and overgrown watercourse.

At the end of the open area, you pass through another little wood, where juniper, cedar elm, and oak trees mingle. To the right, a wooden bridge across the creek leads to Mariposa Drive and out of the greenbelt. The trail continues north toward the Colorado River, coming to Woodland Avenue. Use the pedestrian crossing and then take the trail on the right to follow the creek through a valley that is a reminder of the wildness that once was. Just before you reach Monroe Street, the next cross street, the path splits again. Keep right to go under the stone road bridge. From under the bridge you can look north along the creek, which makes a big horseshoe bend east under thickly wooded limestone bluffs. Follow the trail through the woods, and come out at a field that fills up the horseshoe. It's always a surprise to find this view in the middle of the city.

Typically Austin—an oak tree shades a picnic table at Blunn Creek.

To get to our destination we must cross Blunn Creek, which now veers west on its journey to the Colorado. Little Stacy Park is tucked into the resulting bend, across Sunset Lane. The bridge on East Side Drive has been renamed the Larry Monroe Forever Bridge, in memory of the much-loved local DJ whose radio programs were a big ingredient in the Austin stew. After his death in 2014 more than 300 people contributed money to realize this memorial. Artist Stefanie Distefano has created a mosaic of ceramic records and musical quotes that adorns the bridge parapets.

Once across the bridge, rejoin the trail to enter the leafy enclave of ❷ **Little Stacy Park.** The building to your left is the Little Stacy Park Shelter House, built in 1930 in the Mission style. The architect was likely Hugo Kuehne, who designed shelter houses at many Austin parks. Kuehne was a native Austinite and a founder of the school of architecture at the University of Texas. In 1954 he was named Austin's Most Worthy Citizen for his dedication to Austin public facilities.

At the bottom of the park is a tennis court and the Little Stacy wading pool, which in summer resonates with the sound of children enjoying the water. Tall trees surround the park, making it a secluded treasure. Make your way across East Side Drive at the north end to see the deep channel that Blunn Creek has carved in the limestone. Tall cliffs rise on the northern bank, giving another view of the natural world that lies under and behind the streets and apartment complexes. From here you can retrace your steps to your car, leaving Blunn Creek to find its way to the Colorado River.

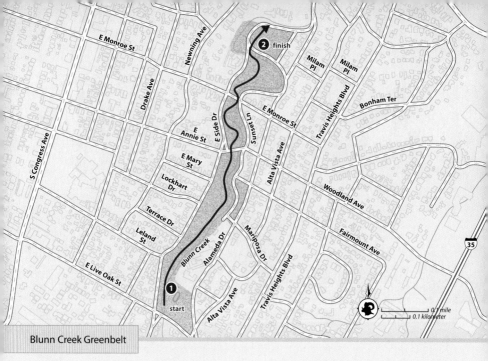

Points of Interest

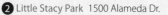

1 Big Stacy Park 700 E. Live Oak St.

2 Little Stacy Park 1500 Alameda Dr.

6 Blunn Creek Nature Preserve Trail
Austin's Volcano

BOUNDARIES: St. Edwards Dr., E. Oltorf St., Little John Lane, I-35
DISTANCE: 1 mile
DIFFICULTY: Moderate
PARKING: Free parking on St. Edwards Dr.
PUBLIC TRANSIT: Bus 801 to stop 5869

Blunn Creek Nature Preserve is an unlikely and somewhat unknown parcel of wilderness that straddles the little creek that flows through the heart of South Austin. Its primitive charms remain uncelebrated in comparison with Zilker Park or Barton Creek. It does not look much like a park from the outside: the northern edge along Oltorf Street appears to be an impenetrable thicket. The main entrance is on St. Edwards Drive, and the dense underbrush does not look too inviting from this southern boundary either. But venture in and you will find a different world, one that is practically oblivious to the neighborhoods that surround it. The short walk through the park takes you past undisturbed canyons full of exuberant fauna and through shadowy woods that are home to

Volunteers help keep the trails looking good at Blunn Creek Nature Preserve.

ancient oaks, their branches bent and black with years. At the high point, there are overlooks with vistas across the preserve to the tower of St. Edward's University. The park is also a time machine, transporting you back 80 million years to when volcanic eruptions formed this topography. At the overlooks you can read informational signs describing the geological processes that created the creek and the canyon through which it flows. Eighty million years ago, when the land was the bottom of an ocean, a volcano erupted, creating a mound of soft volcanic rock called tuff. St. Edwards sits on what remains of this mound. Once the explosions stopped, marine life thrived in the shallower water above the volcano. The creatures' skeletons eventually formed a layer of limestone over the volcanic rock. Ten million years ago, another geological event caused a fault to open up just west of St. Edwards. The tuff east of the fault was covered by hard rock that took a long time to wear away, which is why you can still find pieces of volcanic rock on the eastern side of the fault, including in the preserve. Underground springs flowed through the fault, bursting to the surface as Blunn Creek. Because this is a nature preserve, home to coyotes and other wildlife, dogs are not allowed, and it should be emphasized that this is a short but bona fide hike, not a stroll.

Walk Description

Blunn Creek crosses **❶ Blunn Creek Nature Preserve** diagonally on its way to the Colorado River, entering at the southeastern corner and exiting halfway along the western side. There are two entrances on St. Edwards Drive, on either side of the road bridge over the creek. The 1.5 miles

Backstory: Blunn Creek

Blunn Creek is likely named after an English immigrant, Joseph Blunn, who lived here in the late 1800s and died crossing a bridge in a flash flood. The land was a dairy farm until it was bought by a Lynn Storm in 1952. Thirty years later, Storm wanted to build condos on the tract, but neighborhood associations successfully objected, and eventually the city bought the property from Storm and created the preserve. Blunn Creek is only a few miles long. Its short journey to the Colorado begins under the Walmart on Ben White Boulevard to the south.

of trails in the park make a rough loop with a short but steep detour to the overlooks. At the western entrance a post marked WEST CREEK TRAIL is visible from the street, and that is where we will start. The route disappears into those impenetrable-looking woods. The trails in the preserve are often narrow and overgrown, and in addition are steep and rocky in places, so watch your step. You will immediately come to the next trail marker. Keep left to stay on the West Creek Trail, which makes its way diagonally across the park toward the Long Bow Lane access. The woods are thick with prickly pear, hackberry, and cedar elm, along with Ashe juniper, persimmon, and some huge live oak trees, one apparently more than 450 years old. Volunteers have made great strides in removing invasive plants to allow native plant and animal species to flourish in the wilderness. Squirrels scamper through the branches and dance around tree trunks, and if you pause you might see a rabbit bounding across the trail.

Pass the junction with Blunn Loop, which connects to the East Creek Trail, and then climb up to an open ridge. Look for a sign pointing to the SCENIC VIEW, where a path leads to the edge of the cliff. From here you can take in the picturesque sight of the steep, thickly wooded canyon. Continue to the trailhead at Long Bow Lane and down into the wooded valley, where you cross the creek. As you climb away from the watercourse, you will find the grove of ancient oaks hiding from the modern world in a forest of hackberry, their limbs black and twisted.

Follow the signs to the Overlook, which is at the top of a climb that might have you huffing and puffing. The path comes to a T. Here you will find the first of three vantage points, each surrounded by a low rock wall. Turn left at the junction to find the other two. Each one has another angle on the same vista over the rough terrain, of which the red-and-white tower of St. Edward's University is the most prominent feature. This is where you will find signs displaying the geological information.

Make your way back down the hill you labored up, and go left at the marker and right at the next unmarked fork to follow the East Creek Trail back to St. Edwards Drive. On the way back are a couple of places where you can make your way to the edge of the creek for another look.

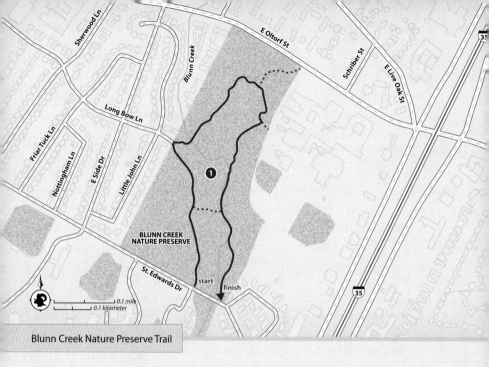

Blunn Creek Nature Preserve Trail

Point of Interest

1 Blunn Creek Nature Preserve 1200 St. Edwards Dr.

7 Boggy Creek Greenbelt
Trees, Trains, and Baseball in East Austin

BOUNDARIES: E. 12th St., Webberville Road, Northwestern Ave., Pleasant Valley Road
DISTANCE: 2.7 miles
DIFFICULTY: Easy
PARKING: Free parking at Rosewood-Zaragosa Neighborhood Center, on Nile St., or at Rosewood Neighborhood Park
PUBLIC TRANSIT: Bus 2 to stop 3932, or bus 300 to stop 1373

This walk explores ❶ Boggy Creek Greenbelt, journeying through the pecan-dotted parkland north of Webberville Road and along the Capitol Metro rail line to reach East 12th Street. The surroundings are a lovely mixture of open fields, wooded groves, and the creek banks, which have been allowed to regain their natural state. On the return journey we will make a detour to the Delores Duffie Recreation Center, a handsome house on a hill overlooking the creek, and the Catherine Lamkin Arboretum, both in Rosewood Neighborhood Park. We will also visit three historic sites, but enjoyment of arboreal variety is the main focus of this ramble through this corner of East Austin. Many different species cover the hillside at the Arboretum, and several majestic pecan and oak trees stand along the creek. The city has planted sycamores and other saplings along the way, has improved the trail, and is restoring the creekside habitat, all of which makes this greenbelt a restful and happy place to spend an hour or so.

Walk Description

The only trail is an easy concrete-and-gravel path along the center of the strip of park that follows a long bend in the creek between Webberville Road and Rosewood Avenue. You can join it anywhere along the route, but we will begin at the southern end by the Rosewood-Zaragosa Neighborhood Center at 2800 Webberville Road. The trail starts right at Webberville Road, by an access ramp that goes down into the creek, which is imprisoned within tall concrete walls (see Backstory, page 38) from here to just past Govalle Neighborhood Park at Bolm Road (see "Southern Walnut Creek," page 149). A metal sculpture stands at the start of the track. Up close it looks like an African mask, covered with vines that are beginning to form a wig.

Walk north, leaving the center to your right. To your left is an unusual sight for an urban area: a thick stand of palmettos bordering the creek channel. A sycamore sapling, one of several newly planted trees, stands in front of them. Follow the sound of falling water to walk to the fenced edge of the channel. Sneak around the palmettos to look at the dam that is the start of the channelized section. Return to the trail, which continues north through the trees, crossing a drainage before coming to the Conley Pavilion. When I last walked here, I found three wooden sculpture pieces with a slightly pagan *Wicker Man* air in this southern section, where people were resting under the shade of the spreading pecans.

A curve in the creek mirrors Nile Street to your left, and the trail makes the first of three water crossings on this walk, entering the more

Some thriving creek ecology along Boggy Creek

open parkland between the rail line and Hargrave Street. A flyover carries Pleasant Valley Road over the railroad and the creek, which mambos east through this area. Pause to study the flora that has been allowed to flourish along the creek banks from the bridge.

Keep right, heading toward the pedestrian crossing at Rosewood Avenue. Go over that street, and stay on the path as it goes under the flyover, alongside the MetroRail line. At some point you will undoubtedly hear the sound of the warning bells from the railroad crossing and see the modern red-and-silver train pass by. Cross the water on a short bridge. At this point Boggy Creek darts west, and a trestle bridge carries the railway over the meandering channel. Enjoy the inspirative sight of thick vegetation along the banks. At the time of writing, the trail is under construction above East 12th Street (the northern end is at East 14th), but we are going to walk as far as we can to take a look at our historical sites. Keep north through a narrow sliver of oak wood between the railroad and the backyards of the houses on Holmes Court. The park soon widens and the trail passes a large pecan tree then crosses the creek for the third time. Another flourish of abundant green lines the banks. Walk through a patch of waste ground and onto East 12th Street. Cross carefully at the railroad crossing and walk east a few steps to the ❷ Downs-Mabson Field, a Texas Landmark whose entrance is adorned with two large murals celebrating the sport of baseball. A historical marker tells of the field's importance as part of the city's African American heritage. Originally built at 12th and Springdale as a "separate but equal" alternative to Disch Field, it was moved to this site—long associated with Huston-Tillotson University—in 1954. During the years of segregation it was a football field for Anderson High, Austin's only African American high school.

This is the northern point of the walk, unless the trail is now open to East 14th Street, in which case completists can follow it up the western side of the baseball field to its end. From here we will retrace our steps, making the two creek crossings and then going under Pleasant Valley Road to come to Rosewood Avenue. Head east along the northern side of Rosewood and cross the railroad, coming to the grand stone pillars at the entrance of Rosewood Community Park. Enter the park and follow the path up a slope toward the house at the top of the hill in front of you. This is the ❸ Delores Duffie Recreation Center, a fine old mansion that has been refurbished and extended to serve as a community center. A Rudolph Bertram bought the house in 1875. He was a local store owner, who passed the property on to his son-in-law, Charles Huppertz. When Huppertz died, the land was sold to the city, which started after-school programs there in 1929. The parks department developed the park in the 1930s, adding tennis courts, the baseball field with its inspiring artwork, and the bandstand at the back of the building. In front of the mansion is a small cabin, another piece of the city's African American history. It was moved here and reassembled in 1973, after the cabin was discovered inside a frame house at 807 E. 11th St. Its owner, Henry Madison, had simply

Backstory: Creekside Controversy

Like most Texas creeks and rivers, Boggy Creek flooded frequently, making life very difficult in the Govalle neighborhood to the west of the park. As a result, after a long campaign, the Army Corps of Engineers channelized nearly 3 miles of the creek in the late 1980s. This severe intervention was typical of the time but would not be allowed today under the city's more enlightened policy to retain as much as possible of the natural character of its creeks. Channelization turns ecosystems into mere drainage channels and stems from a misunderstanding of the natural cycle of flooding. It's a drastic response to the bad human habit of building neighborhoods in flood zones. In addition, channelized creeks become inaccessible, cutting off inhabitants from the benefits of nature. However, the work did stop the flooding, and the subject is a point of contention among newer and older residents of the area.

The problems with Boggy Creek are of course inextricably linked with the city's checkered racial history. East Austin is blackland prairie, where the watercourses have much bigger floodplains than those in the steep and rocky west. As a result of the city's 1928 plan, African American and Mexican American families were forced to move from downtown to the east side and, because of restrictive real estate restrictions, were forced to settle in the floodplain. Whereas Shoal Creek to the west has always been seen as an important ecological resource, Boggy Creek was at best seen as a nuisance of marginal importance. Only after gentrification raised property values on the east side did plans emerge for a restored creek and public access. (The original plan included a bike path, but residents objected, citing privacy concerns.) However, the city and the various neighborhood groups involved deserve kudos for creating this greenbelt, as well as the Southern Walnut Creek Trail, which follows the creek from Govalle Park to Delwau Lane.

built the house around the cabin. Madison lived in this tiny structure with his wife and eight children, so perhaps it is no surprise that he wanted a bigger home.

The last stop on this walk is the ❹ **Catherine Lamkin Arboretum**, dedicated in 1995 and named after a longtime parks department employee. It includes trees from all over the world. See if you can recognize American elm, box elder, or green ash from among the 35 species that cover the slope leading down to the pavilion. Enjoy the shade and the view before you begin the journey back to your parking spot.

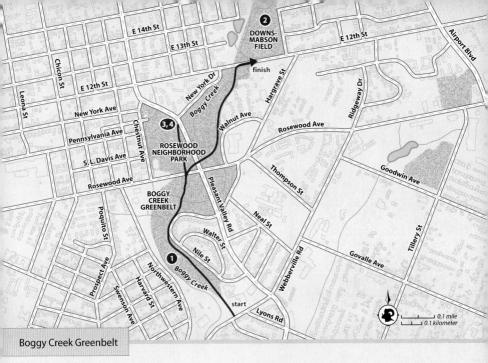

Boggy Creek Greenbelt

Points of Interest

① Boggy Creek Greenbelt 1114 Nile St.

② Downs-Mabson Field 2816 E. 12th St.

③ Delores Duffie Recreation Center 1182 N. Pleasant Valley Road, 512-978-2465, austintexas.gov/department/delores-duffie-recreation-center

④ Catherine Lamkin Arboretum N. Pleasant Valley Road at New York Dr.

8 Bouldin
A Feast in South Austin

BOUNDARIES: Riverside Dr., Newton St., Live Oak St., S. Sixth St.
DISTANCE: 3.5 miles
DIFFICULTY: Easy
PARKING: At Butler Park; behind Dougherty Art Center (2-hour limit); or on street in neighborhood
PUBLIC TRANSIT: Buses 3 and 803 to stop 781

Isaac Decker does not have a street named for him like his southern neighbors William Cannon and Stephen Slaughter, but the land from the river to Williamson Creek (and very roughly between Lamar Boulevard and I-35) was titled to him in 1735, more than 10 years before Austin existed. Much of this parcel ended up the property of Colonel James Bouldin, who came to town in 1850. After the Civil War, Bouldin's freed slaves established communities in the area because rent was cheap due to the constant threat of flooding from the Colorado (see Backstory, page 38), and there are still churches in the neighborhood that were founded by these African American communities. Bouldin's descendants began to sell off the estate after his son David died in the 1890s, and the neighborhood boasts many historic homes from this time, but development really took off in the 1920s and '30s after a rebuilt Congress Avenue bridge opened.

In the 1940s a Hispanic community grew up around the San Juan Diego church. The hippies arrived in the 1970s, Austin's golden years, and the neighborhood still has more than a hint of the smoky (cough) spirit of Old South Austin that was birthed at the Armadillo at the bottom of the hill. Since then Bouldin has drifted slowly upmarket, evidenced by the many designer homes and McMansions that have replaced so many of the original bungalows—topography and location have made it one of the most desirable places to live in the country. But there are still some shacks and casitas, and on South First, mechanics, law offices, and places like La Mexicana and Bouldin Creek Cafe coexist with new coffee shops and swanky eateries like Sway and Lenoir. This walk visits trailers, cafés, restaurants, a historic home or two, and some semisecret wild places on both East and West Bouldin Creeks (yes, there are two). It's a deep dive into this most Austin-y of Austin neighborhoods.

Walk Description

We begin at the ❶ **Dougherty Arts Center** on Barton Springs Road, Austin's oldest community arts center. The Dougherty usually has an exhibition that merits more than a few minutes of your time, but the center's activities go well beyond exhibitions. The DAC has Date Nights (*cumbia*!), youth and adult art classes, summer camps, plays, and movies—there are endless opportunities to marvel or create at Austin's Heart of the Arts.

From the Dougherty Center, cross Barton Springs Road at the light and walk east, savoring the smell of barbecue from ❷ **Terry Black's BBQ**. That's a famous barbecue surname, and the owners are nephews of Kent Black of Lockhart fame. They stumbled at first, getting into a fight with their uncle over the name and then feuding with their Bouldin neighbors about smoke, but things appear to have settled down, and the restaurant has since taken its place in the ranks of Austin's best barbecue joints, which these days (with the exception of Luling's City Market) means the best in the world. My suggestion is to save this one for last; we are going to pass so many great restaurants on this walk, and you can mentally picture a slice of brisket or a piece of banana pudding as a reward to keep you going.

Take the next right on Bouldin Avenue, which runs nearly the length of the neighborhood, from Barton Springs Road to Live Oak Street. We will find out why it does not reach the neighborhood's southern boundary at Oltorf Street when we get there. Keep walking up the steep hill that is the southern bank of the Colorado valley. From Post Oak Street to Christopher Street, Bouldin is only a block wide, sandwiched between the east and west branches of the eponymous creek, and it's easy to see the attraction of a neighborhood with so much nature and a view of downtown, so close you can walk there. Every house has a unique architectural or horticultural element.

Turn left on Christopher, which takes you to the tree-lined edge of the dramatic ravine that contains East Bouldin Creek. Follow South Third south (up the hill), marveling at the homes in this little creekside paradise. After a block you arrive at ❸ Nicholas Dawson Neighborhood Park, to your left. Follow a narrow track into the wooded park, and cross a shallow arroyo to come to the creek channel. Bluffs overlook what would be a lovely swimming hole if the water were clean enough. It's still a beautiful slice of nature sequestered in the heart of the city, so rest for a moment after your exertions climbing the hill. The short park trail connects with a wider, gravel-surfaced track that ends at South First and Gibson just south of the road bridge over the creek.

South First is Bouldin's throbbing commercial center and a major through route; the street sees a lot of rush-hour traffic making its way to and from the neighborhoods south of Ben White Boulevard. The section from the creek to Oltorf Street has so many excellent homegrown restaurants that you could eat here every night for the next month and not run out of meal choices. Kitty-corner to the Gibson junction, to your left, is a lot by the creek where you will see a few food trailers. Walk south almost to Elizabeth Street, where there is a crosswalk to get to the other side of this busy street, and then walk back to the trailers. It is a historic lot, the site of the first Torchy's trailer, which opened in 2006. Torchy's has long gone (it quite soon moved a few yards south to the Trailer Park Eatery), but there's a new contender on the lot, in the Best Indian Food category. In fact the cuisine at ❹ Bombay Dhaba is so tasty, it might be a category-buster. Best item? The Chef's Whim selection, available for lunch in meat or vegetarian versions.

Continue south. At Elizabeth Street look across the street for Cantu's Mexican Imports, where Lee Cantu, a *curandero* (folk healer) from South Texas, practices psychic readings, consultations, *mal de ojo* removal, and other healing treatments. The store is for sale as the Cantus are planning a move to a new location. If it is still there, take what might be your last chance to stop in for pungent herbs and ointments or a religious candle. On this side of South First Street, on either side of Elizabeth you will find Sway and the precious ❺ Elizabeth Street Cafe, both products of modern Austin. Behind its thick hedge, Sway serves modern Thai dishes accompanied by house-made sodas or sake in its swanky, communal-style dining room, while Elizabeth Street Cafe, a (premier Austin restaurateur) Larry McGuire joint that opened in 2011, combines a French boulangerie with Vietnamese cuisine in a cozy cottage whose decor perfectly blends comfortable and formal. For lunch enjoy a Kaffir lime fried chicken bánh mì with an iced Vietnamese coffee on the patio.

There are two food trailers in the lot next door, Mellizoz Tacos and Gourdough's. Mellizoz serves perfectly decent tacos, while Gourdough's (a new Austin staple whose name is a play on the Spanish word for fat) takes donuts to a different place. You probably should have to show a doctor's note before subjecting your body to the sugary delights of a Mother Clucker (donut + fried chicken) or Flying Pig (donut + bacon). Opposite Gourdough's is another of Austin's Moonlight Towers (see "Clarksville," page 51, for more on these towers).

Walk south to Annie Street past an abandoned building, walled in the Mexican style, that is for sale. You may notice the US marshal's NO TRESPASSING notice on the side of the structure. This was Jovita's, a popular, charming, and exuberant Mexican family restaurant that closed overnight when the owners were arrested for running an extensive heroin-dealing network. Next door is the second location of Fresa's, a sit-down version of the downtown drive-through that has expanded the menu to include steak and fish alongside their *pollo Mexicano.*

Annie Street and its neighbor to the south, Mary Street, are the heart of Bouldin, and maybe even of the whole city. Something about the hilly, tree-lined, creek-spanning mixture of houses along these placid streets still embodies the purest essence of what it is to live in Austin. The names (and Eva, Milton, and others) were names of members of the Swisher family, who owned the land before James Swisher subdivided it in the late 1800s. Turn left on Annie, and walk a block to Newton Street, an intersection of contrasts. On the south side of Annie is a typical older white house. On the north side are two town houses that show off the sort of modern designs that have appeared along these streets. And on the northeast corner is the wooden ❻ St. Annie African Methodist Episcopal Church, built in 1915 and part of Bouldin's and Austin's African American heritage. The church is a growing and active member of the Southwest Texas Annual

Even in Bouldin, this house stands out.

Conference, 10th Episcopal District. The AME church organization has served the African American community since the days of slavery.

Retrace your steps to South First and cross the west side of the street. A photo in front of the *Greetings from Austin* mural on the side of Roadhouse Relics is mandatory. This gallery/workshop is where artist Todd Sanders makes his "modern vintage" neon creations that can be found in clubs and homes, on album covers, and in movies and have been acclaimed by the likes of Billy Gibbons and Willie Nelson.

Walk south one more block to Mary Street, passing date-night destination Lenoir. In the little mall to the left is the Soup Peddler, purveyor of delicious soups and juices and a Bouldin original. David Ansel, the peddler himself, began delivering soup by bicycle around the neighborhood in 2002 and opened his first permanent location in 2010. In front of you is ❼ Bouldin Creek Cafe, featuring excellent vegan comfort food, awesome hot tea drinks, and the quintessential low-key Austin vibe. Bouldin Creek Café used to be in a ramshackle multichambered house where Elizabeth Street is, but despite the concerns of the habitual clientele, the menu and atmosphere have been grafted successfully onto this former tire shop that has become one of the city's favorite brunch destinations. Stop in for a tofu and broccoli salad or the yummy Soul Food Plate with red and black beans and collard greens.

Go south one more block on South First to the junction of Johanna Street. Stop in at the Becerra family's ❽ La Mexicana Panadería at any hour of the day or night for *pan dulce,* cakes, tacos, or an economical carnitas plate. You can see the pastries being made behind the counter case that is always full of empanadas, *novias de piña, cuellos de miel,* and much more. And we can't leave South First without a mention for Tex-Mex favorite Polvo's and its mouthwatering salsa bar, just across Johanna Street.

Turn right onto Johanna, and walk west for three blocks to the junction of Bouldin Avenue. Turn left and go to the end of Bouldin Avenue, at

An example of individual style in old Bouldin

Live Oak, one block from Oltorf. The oak-covered grounds of a big white house fill a good portion of the next block. This is the Faulk home, once Green Pastures restaurant and recently reopened as ❾ **Mattie's**, the first piece of a planned boutique hotel, the Faulk. The welcoming Victorian mansion was built in 1894 for a Dr. E. W. Herndon and passed to the Faulk family. It was the boyhood home of John Henry Faulk, the writer and radio personality whose most famous act was to file a lawsuit against Joseph McCarthy's AWARE organization. Faulk won $3.5 million, and the success of the suit was a big step toward ending McCarthy's Hollywood blacklist. His sister Mary Faulk Koock remodeled the family home and opened Green Pastures restaurant here in 1946. It was a big success, and Mattie's, named after John and Mary's mother, continues the tradition of fine Southern dining with a French accent that Mary began.

Walk back down Bouldin Avenue to Mary Street, and turn left. Just before you get to South Fifth and Mary look for ❿ **Thai Fresh** on the left, a coffee shop and Thai restaurant that also sells beer, baked goods, and vegan ice cream. Owner and human dynamo Jam Sanitchat brings passion and precision to the menu and to her cooking classes, where she teaches tricks and tips learned from her grandmother and mother.

Across the street is the indefatigable David's Food Store, which seems to eternally shrug off posher competition. On the southwest corner is the Mary Street Stone House, from the same year as the Faulk mansion (1894) and built by architect and developer Nicholas Dawson as a single-family home. Opposite that is the clean, modern, and well-organized ⓫ **Twin Oaks branch of the Austin Public Library,** designed by hatch + ulland owen and completed in 2010 on the site of an old post office.

Walk north on South Fifth Street six blocks, taking in the widely varying architecture and styles. At Gibson Street, turn left down the hill into the steep valley of West Bouldin Creek. Turn right where the road dead-ends into Sixth Street, and look to your left for the entrance to the ⓬ **West Bouldin Creek Greenbelt.** A short trail takes you through the rugged world along the wooded creek. Take two right turns and you will exit the greenbelt at an apartment complex on Post Oak Street. Before you get to Dawson Street (the name for the northern end of South Fifth) turn to your right for a look at the unusual building that is the High Road on Dawson, formerly an Elks Lodge and now an events center.

Cross Barton Springs Road into Butler Metro Park, and head for the 35-foot high point, named ⓭ **Doug Sahm Hill** in honor of the musician, to take in the 360-degree vista of the city from the skyscrapers of downtown to the wooded rise behind you that is the Bouldin neighborhood. Now you can head to Terry Black's for the promised brisket and banana pudding.

Points of Interest

1 Dougherty Arts Center 1110 Barton Springs Road, 512-974-4000, austintexas.gov/dac

2 Terry Black's BBQ 1003 Barton Springs Road, 512-394-5899, terryblacksbbq.com

3 Nicholas Dawson Neighborhood Park Third and James Sts.

4 Bombay Dhaba 1207 S. First St., 737-247-4323, bombaydhabaaustin.com

5 Elizabeth Street Cafe 1501 S. First St., 512-291-2881, elizabethstreetcafe.com

6 St. Annie African Methodist Episcopal Church 1711 Newton St., 512-444-4509, stannieamec.org

7 Bouldin Creek Cafe 1900 S. First St., 512-416-1601, bouldincreekcafe.com

8 La Mexicana Panadería 1924 S. First St., 512-443-6369, la-mexicana-bakery.com

9 Mattie's 811 W. Live Oak St., 512-444-1888, mattiesaustin.com

10 Thai Fresh 909 W. Mary St., 512-494-6436, thai-fresh.com

11 Twin Oaks branch of the Austin Public Library 1800 S. Fifth St., 512-974-9980
library.austintexas.gov/twin-oaks-branch

12 West Bouldin Creek Greenbelt 1200 S. Sixth St.

13 Doug Sahm Hill Butler Metropolitan Park, 1000 Barton Springs Road

9 Brushy Creek Regional Trail
Wilco's Natural Corridor

Above: Kayakers on Brushy Creek Lake

BOUNDARIES: US 183, Brushy Creek Road, Brushy Creek Lake, Brushy Creek
DISTANCE: 4.5 miles
DIFFICULTY: Easy
PARKING: At Twin Lakes Park or Brushy Creek Lake Park
PUBLIC TRANSIT: 550 MetroRail Red Line to Lakeline Station (a 45-minute walk to Twin Lakes Park)

If you are in North Austin or want to explore somewhere new, try Brushy Creek Regional Trail, which goes from US 183 across Cedar Park and almost reaches Round Rock. Wilco residents flock to this trail to get their nature fix, so much so that the city has posted traffic rules along the route. It's great for walking, cycling, or jogging, and there are wooded groves, open meadows, playgrounds, sports fields, and a lake where you can kayak and fish. The route is nearly 7 miles long, following a branch of Brushy Creek across the city from east to west. There's a trail of the same name in neighboring

Backstory: Williamson County's Beginnings

Sometimes things happen fast. When Austin was founded in 1839, the land around Brushy Creek was home to the Tonkawa Indians and herds of buffalo. Dr. Thomas Kenney built a fort on the creek the same year, and less than 10 years later Williamson County had been established, with its seat at Georgetown. The new arrivals were tough farmers and ranchers whose brutal tenacity beat off Native Americans and Mexicans. Many of them came from Sweden, settling in communities along Brushy Creek on land acquired from the original Swedish Texan, Swen Magnus Swenson. (Swenson's uncle was Sir Swante Palm, Sweden's vice consul who encouraged his countrymen to move to Texas.) Now, though there are still many rural corners to be found, Georgetown, Round Rock, Cedar Park, and Leander are comfortable suburban cities, and overall the county is home to more than half a million people. The Brushy Creek Trail and others like it help to bring these sprawling communities together. As you pass by the strollers and bicycles on this agreeable path, take a moment to remember the county's not too ancient history of horses and cattle, and sweat and blood.

Round Rock, and the plan is to fill in the gap between them in 2019 to create a regional trail system. This walk is presented as an out-and-back promenade from Twin Lakes Park to Brushy Creek Lake Park, though you might choose to shorten or lengthen the route or hike it in reverse.

Walk Description

The smooth concrete path starts at Little Elm Trail to the left of the entrance to the parking lot, following the edge of a patch of woods past the facility's parking lot and the Lower Pool of ❶ Twin Lakes Park. (This 50-acre park operated by the YMCA of Williamson County has swimming, sports fields, and even an archery course.) The trail leaves the park and zigzags across a bridge that spans a rocky channel leading to a waterfall. The banks are festooned with greenery. This is not Brushy Creek, and this walk does not ever come to that creek's main channel. This is South Brushy Creek, and the view from the bridge is of its confluence with Cluck Creek, which flows in from the west. Brushy Creek Trail follows South Brushy Creek until that branch joins Brushy Creek proper at Olsen Meadows Park, which is nearly the end of the Cedar Park section of the trail.

Cross the bridge and enter the thick strip of woods along the creek. The creek bottom is green with dense vegetation, and tall hardwoods press up against either side of the path. A new trailhead under the US 183 toll road is one of the more obvious examples of recent improvements to the facility, though sadly the signs identifying various flora have faded into illegibility. Rocky, juniper-covered terrain surrounds the dense hardwood bottoms, but the landscaped trail undulates smoothly over the rough ground. After about 1.5 miles you will arrive at an open area. After you pass through the meadow, you will see a wooden trestle bridge in front of you. This is the old Austin and Northwestern line to Llano that was used to haul granite to Austin to rebuild the Capitol after a fire destroyed it in 1881. Up until the earlier part of the 1900s the railway was the usual mode of transportation for Williamson County residents. It was normal and convenient to take the train to Austin for an evening's entertainment. Perhaps that will be the practice again, since Austin's Capital Metro owns this railroad.

As you might imagine, the concrete path makes for great cycling, but if you like to go off-road on your bike, there is a maze of singletrack trails waiting for you between the Staked Plains Loop trailhead and the railroad. The most popular, Deception, is 6 miles long and packed with turns and tricky technical features.

The trail continues under the rail bridge and crosses to the north side of the channel, skirting the playing fields at Brushy Creek Sports Park. The creek widens as it approaches the lake. It and the trail go under Palmer Lane and enter ❷ **Brushy Creek Lake Park.** Step over a feeder branch and follow the Lake Creek Loop Trail along the shore. The lake was built in 1965 for flood control and irrigation and is now home to birds such as cormorants, ospreys, egrets, and herons. The wide dam is ahead of you. You will see fishermen on the bank and kayakers on the water, and smell grilling from the picnic tables. Join the steady flow of people on the path across the dam, or perhaps rent a kayak for a paddle on the lake before you head back.

A cyclist rides under the old Austin and Northwestern line.

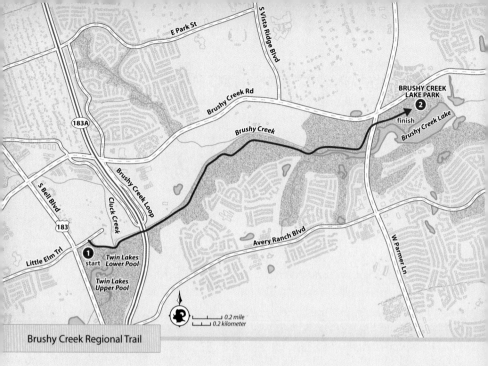

Brushy Creek Regional Trail

Points of Interest

❶ Twin Lakes Park 204 E. Little Elm Trail; 512-250-9622, ext. 6; wilco.org

❷ Brushy Creek Lake Park 3300 Brushy Creek Road, 512-401-5500, cedarparktexas.gov

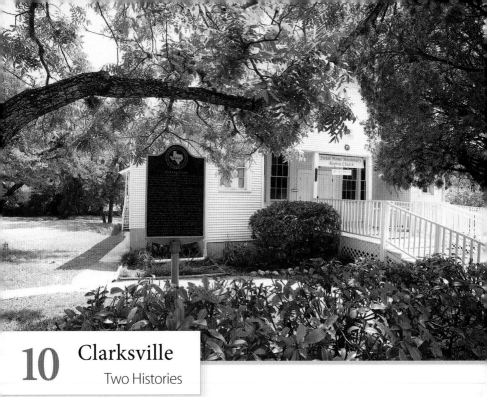

10 Clarksville
Two Histories

Above: *Sweet Home Missionary Baptist Church*

BOUNDARIES: W. Sixth St., Mopac Expy. (TX 1), Waterston Ave., Baylor St.
DISTANCE: 3 miles
DIFFICULTY: Moderate
PARKING: Free parking on Blanco St.
PUBLIC TRANSIT: Bus 4 to stop 2105

On this walk through this prosperous and pretty enclave of old Austin, we will learn something of its history while enjoying the architecture and ambience. The area between Enfield Street, West Sixth Street, Mopac, and Lamar is now known generally as Clarksville, but the original African American neighborhood (and the Clarksville Historic District) consists of the few blocks between 10th Street, Waterson Avenue, Mopac, and West Lynn Street. East of West Lynn is the Anglo part, now the West Line Historic District, named for the streetcar that used to run along Sixth Street. In the 1800s the land above the bluffs west of Shoal Creek (Lamar Boulevard) was a rough plateau covered with dense, impenetrable cane thicket and crisscrossed with steep arroyos that frequently became cascading torrents. It probably felt as remote then as San Angelo does now, so when, after the Civil War, African American leaders petitioned Anglo agents for land, this broken territory out in Indian country must have seemed like a good solution.

Governor Elisha Pease sold the land to Charles Clark in 1871, and Clark established the community that bore his name, which reached its peak in the 1930s, despite the city's repeated attempts to move it. In 1918 they closed the local school, and things came to a head with the infamous city plan of 1928, which codified the city's intent to move all black families to East Austin. The civil rights era ushered in a new plan in 1954, but as late as 1979 Clarksville was still being neglected. Many streets in the neighborhood were unpaved, and drainage was a constant problem. Wastewater and runoff from the Enfield subdivision to the north—one of the first to take advantage of the rise in use of automobiles—caused continual flooding. There was a body blow to the community in 1971 when the Mopac highway took more than a third of its homes. As house prices rose and more people were forced out, residents formed the Clarksville Community Development Corporation, with a mission to preserve historic homes and provide affordable housing. However, the corporation has only 10 properties, and there is a waiting list.

Today only a few homes remain from Clarksville's previous life. This walk will visit some of the historic structures that remain.

Community Garden at the Haskell House

The same year Clark bought his land, the other side of West Lynn Street began to be built up, the development spurred on by the new streetcar line. It was envisioned as a high-class neighborhood, and the first houses were very grand, but over time large lots were subdivided and smaller houses built. The combination of the rough terrain and piecemeal development of the parcels means that the grid pattern is irregular, leading to some odd jogs at street junctures. Like Clarksville, the West Line reached a peak in the 1930s, and the neighborhood has a large number of homes from that time, as well as a few dating back to the late 1800s.

New houses are of course being built, but quite a few of the houses are pleasingly (to the walker, if not the inhabitants) unreconstructed, maintaining the air of gentle slackerdom for which Austin used to be known. The neighborhood has a quietly settled feel, with comfortable homes happily nestled in their almost bucolic surroundings. We will start on West Ninth Street, just above Lamar Boulevard, in the West Line Historic District, and go through old Clarksville to Mopac before returning to the Hope Outdoor Gallery, two blocks from the start.

Walk Description

From your parking spot, find 1112 W. Ninth St., in the block between Baylor and Blanco Streets. Along with West Lynn, Blanco is one of the two main north–south thoroughfares in the neighborhood, and in the 1870s lots along Blanco and along West Ninth began to be carved from the old estates. The ❶ Hauschild-Zerschousky-Watts House at the address mentioned was built in 1905 for Max Hauschild. Three flights of stone steps lead from the pavement to this handsome L-shaped, Queen Anne home, whose porches feature Tuscan columns and a baluster railing.

Walk west to Blanco Street and turn right (north), where there are three houses worth perusal. At 902 is a lovely L-plan Queen Anne with a pretty white picket fence. Two houses up, at 910, the WIlliam Green Hill house is practically unchanged since its construction in 1890. At 1000 Blanco is ❷ Austin Fire Station 4. The 1907 brick building features arched entrances for the engines.

Walk past the fire station west on 10th Street. The street dips down, following the area's rough topography, and at the low point on your left is ❸ West Austin Park, where the paddling pool and bathhouse date from 1935. The low limestone retaining walls on either side give the grassy valley a formal air, almost of an English garden. Walk though the park, built by the city in 1929, to Ninth Street, and turn right past a wooded grove at the western end of the facility, the off-leash area for dogs.

Pause at the junction with Pressler Street. This street was part of the Smoot family holding; they began selling it off as early as 1877, after a new bridge at Sixth Street over Shoal Creek made access to the neighborhood much easier. They had bought the larger holding from James Hervey Raymond, erstwhile state treasurer and entrepreneur, who had built middle-class homes south of West Sixth Street and had sold 5- to 10-acre estates in what was called Raymond Heights north of that increasingly commercial thoroughfare. Paul Pressler's beer garden—in fact, more of a park—between Sixth and the river was a big attraction, though it succumbed to history and was torn up for a subdivision.

The two magnificent residences—the **❹ PIllow Houses**—flanking Pressler Street on the south side of Ninth Street were among the first to be built as a result of the change from country estate to middle-class suburb. The Italianate homes were constructed in 1877–78 for the Pillow brothers, Ben and William, who brought telephone service to Austin. These two-story homes, with their wide porches and balconies, still look fabulous on the little ridge above Ninth. William's house, at 1407 W. Ninth St., was the first in Austin with a telephone and features some outstanding trelliswork.

Keep west on Ninth Street and take the next left, Oakland Street, then the next right, Tremont Street, a short, steep climb up to Highland Avenue, where you turn left. All the homes on this street have some special quality. At 700 Highland is a charming Craftsman/Classical Revival bungalow with sturdy columns and a side porch, and at 617 Highland, a nice Craftsman cottage. Next door to that, at 1412 W. 6½ St. is the **❺ James Raymond Johnson House**, a two-story Italianate mansion built for James Raymond's nephew, another banker. Notice the bay windows and decorative brackets under the eaves. This is one of the few original estate properties left in the neighborhood.

Continue down the hill to Sixth Street. Here we will turn left, heading back to Pressler Street, two blocks away. On the eastern side of the junction of Pressler and Sixth Streets is the huge lot where Richmond Kelley Smoot built his very grand brick home on land bought from Raymond. The **❻ Smoot House** is the only one of the original estate homes that retains its grounds. In the late 1800s all of West Sixth Street was lined with similar houses. Dr. Smoot was a nationally known Presbyterian clergyman who came to Austin from Kentucky. Although we know his home as the Smoot House, he called it Pecan Place, while his wife preferred Flower Hill. One of the building's most notable features, the screened upper porch, was added in 1925.

Retrace your steps along the north side of West Sixth Street, passing Highland Street. Take the next right, West Lynn Street, the neighborhood's other, busier north–south artery. The cell tower at the top of the hill, one of the area's most prominent landmarks, remains visible as you climb. At 610 W. Lynn is the **❼ Sheeks-Robertson House**, another of the original estate homes, built in 1876 by Judge David Sheeks at the end of the horse-drawn trolley line. He had a good view of the Colorado River from the vantage point he chose for his house. The house was extensively remodeled in 1896 by its next owner, Judge Robertson, who came to Austin from Round Rock. Opposite, at 705, is the much more modest Quick bungalow, from 1895. The live oak tree in the front yard decently obscures the fact that the house could use some upkeep.

The neighborhood began growing again in earnest in the early 1900s; bungalows began to fill the subdivisions west of Blanco Street. Taking up most of the 900 block on the west side of the street, **❽ Mathews School** was built in 1916 to serve the burgeoning population—though not the African American children of Clarksville, who went to a different school until desegregation closed that in 1965. It is one of the five oldest public schools in the city.

Pass the school and the cell tower. Take a peek at the two perfect homes at the eastern corner of West Lynn and 10th Street, then turn left on West 10th. You can't help but notice that the houses are smaller and the terrain more difficult as we enter Charles Clark's Clarksville. Walk one (long) block west to the junction with Charlotte Street, where you will find the ❾ Mayes House, a small gray, L-shaped home at 1624 W. 10th. Elias Mayes, a leader of the African American community, moved to Austin in 1884 from Brazos County, where he had been state senator, and bought two lots from Charles Clark here on 10th Street. Mayes's son lived in the house until his death in 1975.

The other side of the street is bounded by an impenetrable thicket of bamboo and foliage. The trees hide a tract with a very different feel from the rest of the neighborhood. Ravines and woods border a large apartment complex, owned by the University of Texas and used as student housing, on a plot whose southern boundary is West Sixth Street. This was the grounds of the Texas Confederate Home for Men, built in the 1880s. The university took over the land in the 1960s after the last veterans died.

Walk west on 10th Street, climbing up the hill on the western side of the UT enclave, passing Toyath Street and Patterson Avenue. The Mary Frances Baylor Clarksville Park is on your right, named after the prominent community organizer and founder of the Clarksville Community Development Corporation. Her efforts helped bring paved streets and a school to this neglected African American community. In front of you is Newfield Lane, the end of the neighborhood, as behind Newfield Lane is the vast Mopac Expressway, the battle to prevent which, as we know, Mary Baylor and the community lost. The sight and sound of the giant freeway is still a shock after the walk through this sequestered little section of Austin.

Go north one block on Newfield Lane, and turn right on West 11th Street, passing the kiddie pool at the other end of the park. At 1725 W. 11th St. is the ❿ Sweet Home Missionary Baptist Church, a focal point and binding force of the community since 1882, when locals began meeting under a shelter at this spot. The white wooden structure that now stands here was built in 1935.

Keep walking east on 11th Street to where it meets Charlotte Street. This is the ⓫ site of Townes Van Zandt's trailer. In the mid-1970s legendary Texas songwriter Townes Van Zandt lived in a mobile home on this corner, on land that belonged to blacksmith "Uncle" Seymour Washington. Apparently, local residents complained about the generally unkempt nature of the property and his "wandering goats." In the outlaw country documentary *Heartworn Highways,* there is a scene where Van Zandt, only slightly drunk, rambles on about life as he wanders around the lot. He cracks the worst joke ever made by a genius, referring to his rabbits as "the bigger, the bunnier."

Go north on Charlotte past the pretty little white cottage at 1104, and turn left at Waterston Avenue. We are heading for the ⑫ Haskell House at 1705 Waterston Ave., possibly the oldest home in Clarksville. It was built in 1879 by Peter Turner, a former slave, who had bought the lot in 1875. The small unpainted board-and-batten home has never been moved and retains much of the original structure. Turner sold the house to the Smith family sometime in the 1880s. Hezekiah Haskell, a buffalo soldier from Baltimore stationed in Texas, married the Smiths' daughter and moved in. His son Hezekiah died in the house in 1976, which was then acquired by the city for preservation. Don't miss the pleasant community garden at the back of the house.

Go east from the Haskell House back to West Lynn Street, where the few sleepy businesses will seem like Times Square after the walk around old Clarksville. Take a right past Jeffrey's Restaurant, one of Austin's oldest and finest dining establishments, heading toward neighborhood landmark the Sledd Nursery sign. Walk across the street to ⑬ Nau's Enfield Drug, admiring the Daniel Johnston mural *Love Is the Question, Love Is the Answer* on the north wall. (Johnston is another much-loved Texas musician, who had his heyday in the 1990s.) Step inside, and immediately you are taken back 30 or 40 years; the decor is unchanged since the store opened in 1951. Order a cheeseburger and soda (from a fountain!) at the counter in back.

From Nau's, go back the few steps to West 12th, and walk east toward downtown. The imposing houses on large lots along this grand street seem worlds away from the hidden neighborhood on the other side of West Lynn Street. One building worth a pause is the unusual Deco-looking house at the junction with Lorrain Street.

At the corner of Blanco Street look for the metal lighting tower. Austinites know these structures as ⑭ Moonlight Towers, and the city's 15 examples are the only surviving working towers in the country. The city acquired them used from Detroit in 1894. They were all completely refurbished in the 1990s, and because this is Austin, that achievement prompted a festival. The towers are on the National Register of Historic Places, as is the house across the street, the 1877 ⑮ Henry H. and Bertha Sterzing Ziller House. The Zillers, both from German families, modified the home in the 1890s, adding the Eastlake ornamentation (named after the English designer) that gives the residence its gingerbread house feel. Subsequent owners restored the home to its 1890s glory in 1993.

Go south on Blanco Street one block, and turn left onto the short section of 11th Street that dead-ends at the top of the bluff called Castle Hill above Lamar Boulevard. At the end of the street on the right is ⑯ The Castle, now a private building whose crenellated tower is the source of its name. It was never a castle, but it was the home of the Texas Military Institute, formerly the

Backstory: Clarksville's Disparate Histories

Leafy Clarksville, a sheltered sanctuary on the hilly plateau west of Shoal Creek, has obviously been prosperous and comfortable for a while. Like Hyde Park, it appears insulated from the troubles of the modern world, and only in a place like this could Nau's, a carefully curated exhibit of a drugstore, exist and thrive for so long. Hylton Nau, a European immigrant, opened his store in the 1950s, and other local stores share almost as long a history—Sledd's Nursery and Jeffrey's restaurant have been going since the '70s. Austin's biggest success story to date began when John Mackay took over the Clarksville Natural Grocery and turned it into Whole Foods. But this successful surface obscures a sadder tale of racism and greed. The charming streets of Clarksville contain many historical landmarks that remind us that even as the tale of old Clarksville fades into the past, the larger story keeps repeating here in Austin and across the United States.

Bastrop Military Institute, started by West Point graduate Robert Allen in 1856. Sam Houston was also a graduate. The school moved to this location in Austin in 1870. The building was supposed to have four towers, but only two were built, and only one survives. The last graduation took place in 1878, after which the building was used by a language school for a while.

Our last stop takes us back to the modern world and is directly below the Castle on Baylor Street. To get there, retrace your steps to 12th Street and turn right. Go down the hill and turn right again on Baylor Street. Halfway along the block is the **17** **Hope Outdoor Gallery**, a graffiti park on the site of a failed condo development officially opened in 2011 with assistance from Shepard Fairey, the artist responsible for the famous "Hope" portrait of Barack Obama. All kinds of colorful works decorate the abandoned foundations that cover the steep lot.

Points of Interest

1 Hauschild-Zerschousky-Watts House   1112 W. Ninth St.

2 Austin Fire Station 4   1000 Blanco St.

3 West Austin Park   1317 W. 10th St.

4 Pillow Houses   Ninth and Pressler Sts.

5 James Raymond Johnson House   1412 W. Sixth ½ St.

6 Smoot House   1316 W. Sixth St.

(continued on next page)

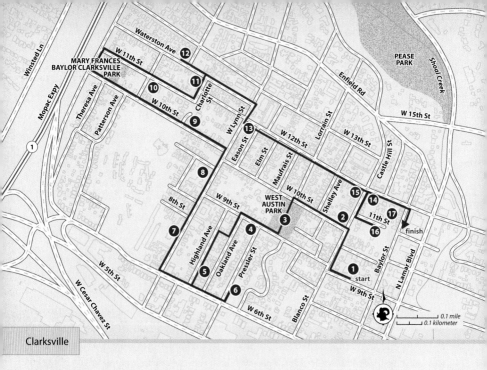

(continued from previous page)

7 Sheeks-Robertson House 610 W. Lynn St.

8 Mathews School 906 W. Lynn St.

9 Mayes House 1624 W. 10th St.

10 Sweet Home Missionary Baptist Church 1725 W. 11th St.

11 Site of Townes Van Zandt's trailer 11th and Charlotte Sts.

12 Haskell House 1705 Waterston Ave.

13 Nau's Enfield Drug 1115 W. Lynn St., 512-476-1221, nausdrug.com

14 Moonlight Tower 12th and Blanco Sts.

15 Henry H. and Bertha Sterzing Ziller House 1110 Blanco St.

16 The Castle 1111 W. 11th St.

17 Hope Outdoor Gallery 1101 Baylor St., hopecampaign.org/hopeprojects/hope-outdoor-gallery

11 Crestview
Midcentury Modern Delight

Above: Enjoy great music and food at Threadgill's, an integral part of Austin's music history.

BOUNDARIES: W. Anderson Lane, Burnet Road, W. Koenig Lane, N. Lamar Blvd.
DISTANCE: 5.5 miles
DIFFICULTY: Easy
PARKING: Free on-street parking on Hardy Dr. by Genuine Joe Coffeehouse
PUBLIC TRANSIT: Bus 5 to stop 1080, or 550 MetroRail Red Line to Crestview. This walk is scooter-
and bike-friendly.

This walk goes off the normal tourist track to discover some lesser-known local emporiums and
eateries scattered around the appealing midcentury Crestview and Brentwood neighborhoods.
These neighborhoods don't have the history of Hyde Park or Travis Heights or the hipster charm
(and McMansions) of Bouldin, but the leafy streets lined with pretty mid-20th-century bungalows are an understated delight. On Woodrow Avenue, known as Church Row, you will see places
of worship of all denominations, more evidence of the neighborhood's tolerant and peaceful

atmosphere. In the 1800s the land belonged to Austin lawyer and legislator John Hancock, and before the Second World War there was a dairy farm here that belonged to Frank and Julia Richcreek, who had come to the area from Weslaco, Texas. Frank died in 1942, and when the war was over, developers established Brentwood and then Crestview (in 1947) on his land. Crestview's developers were Alfred B. Beddow and Ray Yates, who moved the Richcreeks' farmhouse from Justin and Lamar to 1405 Justin Lane, where it still stands. The new subdivisions were at first devoid of trees, and at sunset the violet glow over the western hills was easily visible. It was this glow that gave Austin the nickname The City of the Violet Crown. It's a popular name in both neighborhoods—they have or had the Violet Crown Heights subdivision, the Violet Crown Shopping Center, and the Violet Crown Festival, to name just a few. Crestview does not have a Beddow Street, but it does have Hancock Creek, Yates Avenue, and Richcreek Road. Justin Lane was named for Alfred Beddow's wife. As the neighborhoods were constructed just after the end of the war, many of the early residents were veterans who took advantage of the GI Bill of Rights to purchase new homes. The walk wanders from one excellent eatery to another, so read through and decide where you want to eat lunch or breakfast on the way.

Walk Description

Begin with a coffee and a light pastry at ❶ Genuine Joe Coffeehouse on West Anderson Lane. It's a sprawling, low white building with a comfortable but slightly cramped interior, thanks to the low wooden ceiling. It's a popular place for creatives and coders to get together, and the clientele and the mismatched chairs contribute to the welcoming bohemian atmosphere. They have espresso, smoothies, and edible treats, which you can carry out to the front deck if the weather is accommodating.

Walk south down Hardy Drive through Crestview for two long blocks to the junction with Morrow Street, where Morrow becomes St. Joseph Boulevard. As you walk, you will see a few newer two-story homes, but most of the buildings are the bungalows that still define Crestview. I am particularly fond of the painted brick finish that many of them display. Turn right on St. Joseph, which is, unusually, a divided street with a drainage channel down the center. All the streets to the left are named after saints, perhaps because of their proximity to ❷ Saint Louis King of France Catholic Church, which is to your right, filling the blocks between Hardy and Burnet. Walk all the way to Burnet Road, the eastern boundary of the neighborhood. Turn right and then into the parking lot to find the entrance to the complex. The church has an active congregation, a school, and an early childhood center. Peek into the chapel to admire the high wooden ceiling and bright stained glass, and maybe to say a prayer for digestive stamina.

From the church, head south along Burnet Road, a busy commercial thoroughfare of mostly local businesses that definitely help keep Austin weird. Although new apartment buildings are springing up along the street, Burnet (pronounced with the emphasis on the first syllable) still has much of its funky, Old Austin charm. One of the longest-standing emporiums on the street is ❸ Top Notch Hamburgers, whose sign is one of Austin's best-known landmarks. Its most famous moment is an appearance in Richard Linklater's movie *Dazed and Confused*. The diner opened in 1971, and the charcoal-grilled cheeseburger is still top-notch, as it always has been, and the onion rings are thick and juicy. They have pie.

Next door is the ❹ Austin Furniture Depot, the store that actually does keep Austin weird. If you have stayed in an Airbnb in Austin, you will have undoubtedly noticed an Austin sign hanging somewhere, and probably some colorful metal chairs on the patio. This store is where those come from, and there is much more to discover inside this friendly establishment. A cool cloud of bats decorates the front wall of the building.

Walk south across Richcreek Road to Richcreek Plaza. Whether it's for dessert or energy, you probably need chocolate, so head to the back corner of the mall, where you will find ❺ Chocolaterie Tessa. Look on as owner Tessa Halstead handcrafts her chocolates in small batches using the methods of old European chocolatiers that she learned from her father, Texas chocolate pioneer Rex Morgan. Try a few individual pieces, and perhaps order an assortment box or chocolate cowboy boot to take home to your family.

Keep south and cross Pasadena to find an outpost of another homegrown icon. ❻ Juiceland has been opening new locations (in Houston and Dallas as well) at a rapid rate, and their green-and-orange livery has become a familiar sight around town. Concoctions like the Kaleibrator and the Ninja Bachelor Party have become as much a part of Austin life as the cheeseburgers at Top Notch. Founder Matt Shook got a part-time job making juices in 2001 and never looked back. He started Juiceland in 2011, saying that he wanted his products to refresh his customers as much as a jump into Barton Springs. If you're not thirsty now, choose a bottled juice for later.

Our next stop is a few blocks south on Justin Lane, the boundary between Crestview and Brentwood. Continue down Burnet Road for a long block. You might feel drawn to old favorite Tacodeli or Salty Sow chef Harold Marmulstein's new venture, Tumble 22 Hot Chicken. Perhaps your feet might be telling you to stop in at the Beijing Foot Spa. When you reemerge, keep going south and make a slight left onto Burnet Lane, following it down to Justin Lane. Kitty-corner is a strip mall where you find ❼ Lala's Little Nugget, where it is always Christmas. For years this place was a true Austin secret, a bar where the red lights would shine on redder faces, but it has changed hands and undergone some judicious refurbishment. Miraculously it retains the brown carpet and shabby ambience of the old joint while providing a welcoming atmosphere for new-comers. Try a signature Bloody Mary, or choose from the rotating cast of beers on tap.

Should you care to leave Lala's and continue, go east along Justin Lane and turn right on Yates Avenue, then cross the street to enter **❽ Brentwood Neighborhood Park**, the only public green patch on this walk. Follow the path south and then left through the park to come to Arroyo Seco. Turn right. Keep south on Arroyo Seco 10 blocks, all the way to West Koenig Avenue. Brentwood residents began planting trees along the street in 1992, and their Crestview neighbors have done the same north of Justin Lane. Now these saplings provide color and shade for walkers and cyclists, making this one of the most pleasant sections of this route. The north and south lanes run on either side of Hancock Creek, part of the Shoal Creek watershed. When the neighborhood was first devel-oped, this swampy creek made travel along the unpaved streets difficult, so the Lester family, local residents who owned a construction company, dug out this deeper channel.

Cross Koenig Lane, a busy east–west thoroughfare, and turn left, going east for a block to the Brentwood location of **❾ Thunderbird Café and Tap Room**. Their coffee is from roasters Wild Gift Coffee in Round Rock, Texas, and Counter Culture Coffee in North Carolina, and they offer a selection of local beers. In the morning they have Tacodeli tacos.

Sample some of Texas's best barbecue at Stiles Switch BBQ in the Violet Crown Shopping Center.

From Thunderbird Café go east along Koenig across Woodrow and past an abandoned car lot, the least attractive section of this walk. The tall building ahead of you is the McCallum High School Arts Center. Turn right at Grover Avenue, cross a bridge over an unnamed creek, and then turn right into the parking lot of ❿ **Dart Bowl**. This perennially popular bowling alley boasts 32 lanes that have been remodeled with automatic bumpers and scorers. Jerry and Betty Ray opened Dart Bowl in 1958 at Anderson and Burnet and then took over what was Capitol Bowl on Grover in 1996. The bonus is the alley's café (which has been featured on the Food Network); the enchiladas in particular have gained celebrity status. Opened by Butch Martinets and Peggy Vamarripa in 1970 at the old location, the café moved along with the business. They have a full bar and a traditional menu that includes breakfast and chicken-fried steak along with the Tex-Mex fare. The bowling alley is a popular place for parties and corporate gatherings, but there's usually a lane open, so rent some shoes and a lane, and earn your enchiladas!

The next section of this route takes us up busy Lamar Boulevard along the west side of Crestview. This eclectic and slightly seedy strip is one of my favorite bits of Austin. Walk north on Grover across Koenig and take the first right, Romeria Drive. Climb the short hill up to Lamar Boulevard, where you turn left. Look for the ⓫ **Heo Eatery** on the left, which lacks ambience but serves extremely tasty Vietnamese street food. Try the Pork Rib Rice Box or a Roasted Chicken Bao. One block north, just past the Richard Lord Boxing Gym, you will come to ⓬ **Threadgill's Restaurant**, the most famous stop on this walk and an integral piece of Austin's legendary music scene. Eddie Wilson, who ran the Armadillo (see page 19), bought Kenneth Threadgill's old beer joint in 1980 after the Armadillo was torn down. Wilson brought his famous Southern-style cooking north, so get ready to chow down on pork chops, po'boys, or the famous chicken-fried steak. Legend has it that Threadgill, a bootlegger and music fan, stood in line all night to get the first beer license issued in Travis County after Prohibition. His gas station in far north Austin became the go-to place for pickers and singers looking for a drink after their show. Local musicians began to show up, including Janis Joplin, who packed the place every Wednesday night with the Waller Creek Boys and was stunned to realize that people were driving out to the joint just to hear her. Although times have moved on, you can still hear great music and eat great food in a convivial atmosphere at Threadgill's.

Keep north on Lamar, eyes straight ahead as you pass the Yellow Rose, the strip club that for nearly 30 years has been one of the city's more lubricious icons and that—I'm told—serves decent steaks. Stop and take a photo of the giant Centennial Liquor sign. Cross Brentwood Street and look for ⓭ **Stiles Switch BBQ** in the historic Violet Crown Shopping Center.

Volumes have been written about the finer points of Central Texas barbecue, so we'll keep it brief: even though Stiles is not Luling City Market, it is one of Austin's best smokeries. The tasty tender brisket and the beef chuck ribs are good choices. For sides, go with the potato salad and corn casserole.

Onward and upward to the last two stops on Lamar before we turn back west. Look for some more Old Austin landmarks as you go. The old Texan (formerly Waldorf) Motel has a fresh coat of orange-and-white paint and looks ripe for hipster takeover, unlike its shabbier neighbor Mehl's. At the back of the Centennial Plaza is the Korean ⓮ Han Yang Market, whose motto is "Competition in Good Faith. "They carry all kinds of things you can't get at H-E-B, like proper tofu, different types of ginseng, and dried fish. They also have gift cards, which might make great presents for your more gastronomically adventurous Austin friends.

The last place on this northward trek offers a chance for a rest before we tackle the last leg. ⓯ Black Star Co-op is in a new building just past Crestview Station. Cross the rail tracks and enter the plaza to find the entrance around back. This brewpub opened in 2010 and was the first to be cooperatively owned by its members, so you can enjoy your craft beer knowing that you are supporting livable wages (there's no tipping) and a democratic workplace. Pick your poison from the Rational list of mainstay brews, or go out on a limb with a seasonal Irrational. Pair your brew with some tasty fish and chips or a Black Star burger.

Leave Black Star and head south on Lamar a few steps before turning right on Justin Lane. As mentioned, this is the official border between Brentwood to the south and Crestview to the north, even though the section of Brentwood between Koenig and Lamar feels more like a different neighborhood. Walk two long blocks to Woodrow Avenue, and then a couple more steps to pay homage to the ⓰ Richcreek House at 1405 Justin Lane. (The Richcreeks were the dairy farming family from whom the land that is now Crestview was purchased, and this house was moved from Justin and Lamar by the original developers.)

Our last three stops are all at a small mall on Woodrow Avenue. Walk back to Woodrow and walk north until you come to the low brick shopping center. ⓱ Arlan's Market is a 10-aisle neighborhood grocery, unremarkable except for the fact that until 2016 it was the Crestview Minimax IGA, a 1950s-era store that inspired fierce devotion from locals and won several Best of Austin awards. Walk across the plaza to ⓲ Top Drawer Crestview. This thrift store benefits Project Transitions, a charity that since 1988 has provided accommodation for people living with AIDS at Central Texas's first residential hospice, known as Doug's House. Next door, and the last stop on this tour, is the marvelous ⓳ Little Deli & Pizzeria, which is little, though their truly great New York–style sandwiches and pizzas are not. Try Harry's Perfect Pastrami or a Meatball Sub, and try

Stop in for a Bloody Mary at Lala's Little Nugget, where it's always Christmastime.

to save room for a homemade brownie. If you can still walk after so many gastronomic delights, the route back to the starting point is to go north on Woodrow five blocks, turn left on Morrow Street, then go right on Hardy Avenue to come back to Anderson Lane. Or you could summon an Uber to take you home.

Points of Interest

1. Genuine Joe Coffeehouse 2001 W. Anderson Lane, 512-220-1576, genuinejoecoffee.com
2. Saint Louis King of France Catholic Church 7601 Burnet Road, 512-454-0384, st-louis.org
3. Top Notch Hamburgers 7525 Burnet Road, 512-452-2181, topnotchaustin.com
4. Austin Furniture Depot 7511 Burnet Road, 512-323-5222, austinfurnituredepot.com
5. Chocolaterie Tessa 7425 Burnet Road, 512-200-2837, chocolaterietessa.com

(continued on next page)

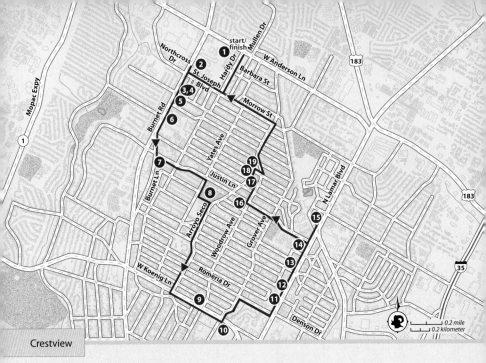

(continued from previous page)

6 Juiceland 7329 Burnet Road, 512-524-1129, juiceland.com

7 Lala's Little Nugget 2207 Justin Lane, 512-487-5297, lalasaustintexas.com

8 Brentwood Neighborhood Park 6710 Arroyo Seco, friendsofbrentwoodpark.org

9 Thunderbird Café and Tap Room 1401 W. Koenig Lane, 512-420-8660, thunderbirdcoffee.com

10 Dart Bowl 5700 Grover Ave., 512-452-2518, dartbowl.com

11 Heo Eatery 6214 N. Lamar Blvd., 512-243-5906, heoeatery.squarespace.com

12 Threadgill's Restaurant 6416 N. Lamar Blvd., 512-451-5440, threadgills.com

13 Stiles Switch BBQ 6610 N. Lamar Blvd., 512-380-9199, stilesswitchbbq.com

14 Han Yang Market 6808 N. Lamar Blvd., 512-371-3199, austinhanyangmarket.com

15 Black Star Co-op 7020 Easy Wind Dr., 512-452-2337, blackstar.coop

16 Richcreek House 1405 Justin Lane

17 Arlan's Market 7108 Woodrow Ave., 512-459-6203, arlansmarket.com

18 Top Drawer Crestview 7101 Woodrow Ave., 512-454-8646, topdrawerthrift.org

19 Little Deli & Pizzeria 7101 Woodrow Ave., Ste. A, 512-467-7402, littledeliandpizza.com

12 Downtown
Edwin Waller's Vision

BOUNDARIES: Red River St., 12th St., Nueces St., Lady Bird Lake
DISTANCE: 4.5 miles
DIFFICULTY: Moderate
PARKING: In the city lot behind the MACC at 600 River St.
PUBLIC TRANSIT: Bus 17 to stop 995 to get to the MACC, but most routes go through downtown. This walk is scooter- and bike-friendly.

Judge Edwin Waller came to Texas in 1831 from Missouri and joined the struggle for Texas independence. After the Texians' victory, he was sent by President Mirabeau Lamar to set up a new Texas capital. He drew a simple 1-square-mile grid to be set between Waller and Shoal Creeks on the banks of the Colorado. The judge himself conducted the first auction for lots in 1839 under the oaks at what is now called Republic Square, and he went on to be Austin's first mayor. Time has vindicated Lamar and Waller's choice. The grid remains, though Judge Waller might recognize but one or two buildings, and some of the old shines on in the shadow of the new skyscrapers.

Walk Description

The distinctive white building on River Street is the ❶ Emma S. Barrientos Mexican American Cultural Center, where we begin this walk. Designed by renowned Mexican architect Teodoro González de León, the center opened in 2007. It is dedicated to preserving and promoting Latino culture, and there is always something to enjoy here, be it an art exhibition, a film festival or documentary showing, a musical event, or just an admiring walk around the striking structure. One of the center's most successful ventures is the Latino Arts Residency Program, which supports groups like Aztlan Dance and ProyectoTeatro. The works these groups produce aim to reflect and inspire the Latino community while providing insight into the Latino experience.

Go east on River Street, and then turn left onto Rainey Street. Zoned commercial in 2005, this established Mexican American neighborhood was transformed almost overnight into party central, with every house made into a bar. Now, upscale hotels, restaurants, and condos have moved in, giving the street a touch more sophistication—or maybe the same people just get drunk on more expensive drinks. Stop in for a beer and a gourmet sausage at Bangers or a cocktail at Half-Step, or pay respect to the granddaddy of the Rainey scene, Clive Bar, at the corner of Davis Street, where you can score mezcal in the supposedly secret courtyard bar. Turn left on Davis.

Next door to Clive Bar is the spiffy new Hotel Van Zandt. This boutique tower is home to one of Austin's most fun brunch experiences. Take the elevator to the fourth floor to find ❷ Geraldine's, where the views and the slightly clubby but seriously hip atmosphere are the perfect backdrop for the Southern-inspired cuisine and seductive cocktails. The restaurant is named after a guinea fowl who used to roam the neighborhood.

Back on Davis Street, turn left and then right onto Red River Street. Walk north past the parking lots to East Cesar Chavez Street, formerly First Street and once Waller's Water Avenue, the southern boundary of the original plat. The towers of the new downtown crowd the view to the left over the Convention Center. Take a moment to admire the brand-new Fairmont, a sleek two-part glass slab with more than 1,000 Gensler-designed rooms that is Austin's biggest hotel. Cross Cesar Chavez Street and continue on Red River to pass ❸ Ironworks BBQ, which is usually crammed with tourists and conventioneers. The name is not some macho take on the restaurant's smoking skills. Fortunat Weigl (whose house you can visit on the Hyde Park walk, page 95) was another German lured to Texas by tales of the cowboy life. He set up his ironworks here in 1935, immediately enduring a historic flood, but he and his sons persevered and went on to craft pieces that grace many of Austin's homes and public buildings. The weathervane on top of the restaurant was made by Weigl's son Lee.

East Avenue, logically enough, was the eastern edge of Edwin Waller's grid. That street was obliterated by I-35 in the 1950s, so we will continue north on Red River. Waller Creek snakes down to the river between Red River and the highway, and at the time of writing it's a mostly inaccessible strip of trashed-out nature. A new tunnel has apparently not solved the flooding problem. But the city is proceeding with an ambitious plan for a string of parks along the creek, and some of the first signs of what is going to be a really nice amenity are visible on the bend between Cesar Chavez and Red River, at the corner of the convention center. The creek cuts through Sir Swante Palm Neighborhood Park, to your right, once a useful connection between East Austin and downtown but now a sad scrap of land that the Waller Creek Plan looks to transform. Palm was the Swedish vice consul in the mid-1800s, an erudite man who made a lasting contribution to Texas's development, in no small part by encouraging many of his fellow countrymen to move to Texas. Austin would be a very different city today without the Swedes, in particular because South by Southwest, its most famous attraction, was started by Roland Swenson, an Austin native of Swedish descent.

The Independent, known as the Jenga Tower

Turn left on East Sixth Street. Dirty Sixth is the name that the city's collective consciousness has birthed for the beery blocks between Brazos Street and I-35. The discriminating left long ago for the joints on the other side of I-35 (see "East Sixth," page 81), leaving Dirty Sixth to those who like their revelry a little more unabashed—though there is currently a cocktail bar resurgence around Congress Avenue. The old Victorian storefronts that sprang up along the easiest route across town are still here and worth seeing in daylight. The Italianate E. H. Carrington Grocery Store at the northwest corner of Red River and East Sixth was one of several African American–owned businesses on the strip.

Make your way along East Sixth until you come to the ❹ Driskill Hotel at the corner of Brazos Street. The striking, castlelike limestone building is from 1886 and was designed by Joseph N. Preston and Son of Austin. Jesse

Driskill came to Austin from Missouri and made his fortune from beef, making him a bona fide cattle baron. He wanted the "best hotel south of St. Louis," and he got it. An ad supplement in the Daily Statesman gushed, "What a Bonanza Austin possesses in its new caravansary" and correctly forecast a rosy future for the city as a tourist mecca. Walk through the grand Sixth Street entrance into the immense pillared lobby, and take a lungful of old money. Continue up the staircase in front of you to the luxurious Driskill bar, where you should take a moment or two to relax into the comfortable buzz of this historic room.

Leave the hotel by the bar entrance and walk north on Brazos Street, past the Central Presbyterian Church and, between Ninth and 10th Streets, St. Mary's Cathedral. Cross 11th Street into the grounds of the Capitol. Let's start at the **5** **Texas Capitol Visitors Center,** the three-story building at the southeast corner of the grounds. Once the General Land Office, this is the oldest state building in Texas. After a period when it fell into disrepair, it was reborn as the Visitors Center in 1994. Its grand appearance speaks to the importance of land in the Texas of the late 19th century. William Porter (O. Henry), whose name crops up a lot in stories of Austin (and in this book), worked here as a draftsman, and the tools he used are on display.

The **6** **Texas Capitol** itself was built in the 1880s by Gustav Wilke. The current structure is the fourth Capitol building and was modeled after the national Capitol in Washington (except bigger, because Texas). Wilke had some problems: he was subcontracting the job from Abner Taylor, who

The Butler Trail in East Austin

fought with the state about the cost of the red granite and controversially got convicts to cut the stone. Wilke imported "illegal" Scottish granite workers and got the job done, though he had to come back and patch the leaking roof. Capitol tours are available and well worthwhile; choose from 1 hour, 2–3 hours, and half a day. Various memorials are scattered around the grounds, including the new African American Memorial Monument on the South Lawn, which was erected in 2016.

Leave the Capitol grounds by the northwestern exit at Colorado and 13th Street. The Victorian-style white building opposite was a grocery store belonging to German Joseph Goodman. It served the inhabitants of northern Austin, including German sculptor Elizabet Ney, who rode her horse here from Hyde Park. The dive bar in the basement, the Cloak Room, has been a favorite of legislators and state employees since it opened in the 1970s and has undoubtedly seen more wheeling and dealing than any other spot in Texas, even the Driskill bar.

From the Cloak Room, head south on Colorado past the vast First United Methodist Church, built in the 1920s. You might have seen its dome from 12th Street as you approached the Capitol. Across 11th Street is the next stop, the ❼ Governor's Mansion. Turn downhill (east) and then right to walk in front of the stunning mid-19th-century Greek Revival–style home. The six Ionic columns and veranda have been the backdrop for countless balls and receptions. Free tours are scheduled for Wednesdays, Thursdays, and Fridays, 2–4 p.m., but you must reserve a space online.

Walk east down the steps opposite the entrance to the mansion through a parking lot to Congress Avenue. Plaques along the way commemorate famous Texans. At Congress turn right into the Congress Avenue Historic District. The first building you passed (on the west side of the street) is Charles Lundberg's Bakery. Lundberg was a Swede who bought out his employer and constructed this building. The installation of the eagle on the rooftop got him a mention in the paper. This stunt proved successful, as his baking skills matched his publicity skills, and his wares became very popular.

Keep walking south on the west side of the street. The building at Ninth and Congress is on the site of Sir Swante Palm's library, which also served as the Swedish consulate. The Art Deco sign on Kruger's Jewelry Store at Eighth Street is from the late 1940s. In the same block across the way are the historic Stateside and Paramount theaters, which play host to Hollywood stars, famous musicians, and local favorites. The Paramount's blade, as the huge sign is called, is a faithful copy of the original, which was lost in 1963. The replacement was erected in 2015 to mark the theater's 100th anniversary.

At Congress and Seventh, pop into the renovated ❽ Jones Center, one of the Contemporary Austin's two locations. The gallery brings interesting work from all over the world to Austin's only downtown showcase for contemporary art. Cross Seventh Street and turn right to continue

The Governor's Mansion

west on the south side of West Seventh Street, to better study the **9** **Norwood Tower**, which is at 114 W. Seventh. At eye level it is a very pretty bank, but if you look up you will see why Lady Bird Johnson called it the "most beautiful building in Austin." At one time only the Capitol was taller. It was built in 1929, and the Johnson family bought it in 1997. Looking like a wedding cake or fairy-tale castle, the romantic Gothic Revival tower is covered with tracery, foliated ornament, and even gargoyles.

The most beautiful building in Austin is actually the **10** **John Bremond House**, on the corner of Seventh and Guadalupe, two blocks west of the Norwood. *Stunning* is not a strong enough word for this house, part of a row of gorgeous buildings set on a bluff that must have overlooked half the city. Elaborate but perfectly proportioned, the lovely Victorian building is in the Second Empire style, which was inspired by French architecture from the time of Napoléon III. The iron-work on the two-story veranda is delightfully well crafted. John Bremond and his brother Eugene were bankers and socialites in late 19th-century Austin. They built or remodeled the houses in this and the adjoining blocks for themselves and family members, creating the unique architectural enclave. Next door to the John Bremond House is the Pierre Bremond House, and beyond that, Eugene's residence. Walk around the corner to San Antonio Street to find the Catherine Robson house, and on the corner, the Walter Bremond house. On the other side of San Antonio Street is the North-Evans Château, remodeled by architect Alfred Giles in 1894. Take your time to savor the oldest cluster of buildings in Austin, then walk back to Seventh and Guadalupe, where, on the south side of the junction, there is a pretty single-story building from the 1850s. This is the B. J. Smith house, an example of a "common" house of the era.

On the next part of the route we will traverse a part of downtown that is currently undergoing radical change. Keep south on Guadalupe Street two blocks until you reach the northeast corner of ⑪ Republic Square, included in Waller's original plan as Hemphill Park. For many years it was a parking lot but has undergone extensive renovation and is now a delightful space where art and shade encourage a change of pace. Relax and enjoy the views of the ever-changing city.

From the opposite end of Republic Square, go west on Fourth Street, and turn left on Nueces, where new buildings have shot up seemingly overnight. Turn right on Second Street. This section of Shoal Creek has received a complete makeover: in front of you is the lovely new Butterfly Bridge, and on the other side of the creek, the new ⑫ Austin Central Library, which stands over a redesigned creekside walkway. Austinites are still oohing and aahing about this new facility. Entrance is free. Take the elevator to the library's roof garden for views over Lady Bird Lake and downtown. Designed by Texas firm Lake/Flato, the library and grounds contain many permanent art pieces, including the popular grackle clock, a sculpture by Christian Moeller titled *CAW,* which hangs in the atrium.

Exit the library and join the trail along Shoal Creek. We will follow this lakeside trail back to the starting point. Walk under the Cesar Chavez Street bridge, and then turn left, along the spur that has built up where the creek enters the river. A bridge connects the spur to the main bank, and to the Ann and Roy Butler Hike and Bike Trail. Turn left to go east, under the South First Street and Congress Avenue bridges. You will smell the guano from Austin's famous bats, which live here in the summer. Pass the steep lawn behind the Radisson hotel, and walk behind the Waller Creek Boathouse, home to the Austin Rowing Club, Congress Avenue Kayaks, and Alta's Café.

Just past the boathouse, you will find one of the Contemporary Austin's most spectacular exhibits. Chinese artist and activist Ai Weiwei's *Forever Bicycles* is a steel arch of hundreds of bike frames. The trail bends to the right past stone lagoons and crosses the end of Waller Creek. There's a trail junction, where the dirt path straight ahead of you leads back to the parking lot behind the MACC.

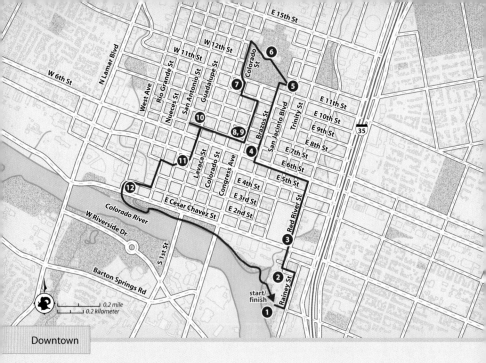

Points of Interest

1 Emma S. Barrientos Mexican American Cultural Center 600 River St., 512-974-3772, austintexas.gov/esbmacc

2 Geraldine's 605 Davis St., 512-476-4755, geraldinesaustin.com

3 Ironworks BBQ 100 Red River St., 512-478-4855, ironworksbbq.com

4 Driskill Hotel 150–172 Sixth St., 512-439-1234, driskillhotel.com

5 Texas Capitol Visitors Center 112 E. 11th St., 512-305-8400, tspb.texas.gov

6 Texas Capitol 1100 Congress Ave., 512-463-4630, tspb.texas.gov

7 Governor's Mansion 1010 Colorado St., 512-463-5518, tspb.texas.gov

8 The Contemporary Austin–Jones Center 700 Congress Ave., 512-453-5312, thecontemporaryaustin.org

9 Norwood Tower 114 W. Seventh St.

10 John Bremond House 700 Guadalupe St.

11 Republic Square 422 Guadalupe St., 512-381-1147, republicsquare.org

12 Austin Central Library 710 W. Cesar Chavez St., 512-974-7400, library.austintexas.gov

13 East Austin
BBQ, Churches, and History

Above: *Gardens at the Texas State Cemetery*

BOUNDARIES: I-35, E. 12th St., Rosewood Ave., E. 11th St.
DISTANCE: 3 miles
DIFFICULTY: Easy
PARKING: On-street parking on San Marcos St. or Juniper St.
PUBLIC TRANSIT: Bus 2 to stop 657

What is now called East Austin first boomed in the late 1800s when the railroad arrived, and the Victorian mansions still standing on Cesar Chavez Street are a reminder of this era (see "Tejano Trails," page 159). At that time much of the city's African American and Mexican American populations lived downtown and along East Avenue (which was obliterated by I-35), and "East Austin" meant east of Congress. This arrangement ended in 1928, when, in the grip of the new "social sciences," the city determined to move these communities to the east side. It achieved this by moving the services available for them. For example, the first race-based public housing projects in the nation were built over here. Mexican families mostly migrated to the lower East Side, while black people moved into the neighborhoods around 11th and 12th Streets and farther north. For a while this area flourished in its own way, but in the 1950s I-35 cut off the communities to its east completely, and with the promise of the civil rights era, people began to look for a better life elsewhere. East Austin began the decline into the ghetto that it became in the 1980s. These changes killed the black blues scene, and the sound of Austin became the sound of the Vaughan brothers—Jimmie and Stevie Ray—though they themselves always credited Austin's blues roots. In the '90s things started to change. The Austin Revitalization Authority, a quasiprivate organization dependent on city money, started to build some houses and try to bring a sense of pride and community back to the area, but sadly they have failed to bring back the African American business community, and most of the new businesses in the area are Anglo-owned. Though East 11th Street is buzzing again, it's mostly because of the influx of new residents. On this walk we will visit some of the sites associated with the neighborhood's African American history and then end up at two sites of more general historical significance. But to begin, there will be barbecue, and more along the way.

The Southgate-Lewis House

Walk Description

Get up as early as you like to join the line at ❶ Franklin Barbecue, which opens at 11 a.m. However early you arrive, someone will be in front of you, so be prepared to wait a couple of hours. It's worth the wait to taste what I and thousands of happy customers agree is the best barbecue in America. Slather on the espresso sauce to stay awake for this walk.

Waddle west a few steps toward I-35 for a look at the arch put up in the 2000s by the Austin Revitalization Authority. It marks the entry to East Austin, and the design represents a symbolic link between the neighborhood and downtown, implicitly acknowledging the city's decades of ignoring the black and brown communities of East Austin. Eleventh and 12th Streets have changed dramatically, with new houses and business appearing in the heart of Austin's African American neighborhood, whose history the community is fighting to remember and preserve in the face of gentrification and rising property values.

Walk east, and cross to the south side of East 11th to visit the ❷ Texas Music Museum. This cramped institution is stuffed full of interesting and cool artifacts from all kinds of artists. Rotating exhibitions explore the many traditions of Texan music, from gospel to conjunto to country. As you would expect, there is a permanent exhibition dedicated to the contributions of African American artists. Even if the sweet sounds of Texas are not new to your ear, you will surely learn something new about the Music Professors and the Victory Grill. And if they are new to you, this is a great place to start. I watched a man (from out of state, surely) earnestly writing down Doug Sahm's name.

From the museum, head south on San Marcos Street to the end of the block for a look at the first of the churches on this walk. This solid-looking building is the ❸ Ebenezer (Third) Baptist Church, whose congregation first built a church on this lot in 1885; the current edifice is from 1915. Return to East 11th Street and turn right. At the end of the block is the Dr. Charles E. Urdy Plaza. Urdy, a respected figure in the community, is chairman of the Austin Revitalization Authority and served as mayor pro tem in the 1990s. The plaza features murals by local artists John Yancey and Regina Thomas. Just behind the plaza is the Bailetti-Walker House, a charming bungalow, and at the corner of 10th and Waller is the Metropolitan African Methodist Episcopal Church, another church founded in the 1880s that continues to play an uplifting role in the community. The current building is from 1922.

Walk back to 11th Street, cross it, and turn right. We next visit the site of the ❹ Victory Grill, one of the most important repositories of Austin's African American history. This historic music venue was an important stop on the famous Chitlin' Circuit of clubs, where black performers could play safely. Legends like Bobby "Blue" Bland, B. B. King, and Clarence "Gatemouth" Brown, and local blues stars like T. D. Bell and W. C. Clark all played here regularly. Bland's last show here was as recent as 2001. Sadly the club is now closed, and its future seems uncertain, though it remains in the original owner's family.

Local promoter and historian Harold McMillan keeps the Victory spirit alive—for the moment—next door at Kenny Dorham's Backyard, an amphitheater where you can often hear music and where there are always trailers serving African, Jamaican, and other tempting food. Continue to the lights at the intersection of 11th and Rosewood Avenue, where the Quickie Pickie serves as a hangout and casual eatery for East Side residents. Take a break on the patio with a taco or sandwich and some of the excellent coffee. Or, for brunch and oysters, visit the Hillside Farmacy across the street.

Walk up Rosewood Avenue. The historic mansion at the junction of 11th is the Haynes-DeLashwah House, a Queen Anne–style home from 1890 that overlooks 11th Street and downtown. It is now ❺ Rosewood, a stylish new restaurant that features an adventurous menu by chef Jesse DeLeon inspired by the cuisine of South Texas.

Turn left on San Bernard Street, and find the ❻ Wesley United Methodist Church at the end of the block. As the sign will tell you, the congregation was established after the Civil War for freed people, who held their first official meeting on March 4, 1865. It was the mother church for the historic African American West Texas Conference and was long associated with Huston-Tillotson University. The church purchased this lot in 1929 and moved from the impressive edifice known as "Wesley on the Hill" at Ninth and Neches.

Go right (east) on Hackberry Street. On the left look for the ❼ Church of God in Christ #1, a member of the Church of God in Christ, the largest Pentecostal denomination in the United States, headquartered in Memphis. Across the street is the ❽ George Washington Carver Museum, which focuses on African American culture. For more neighborhood history, look for the permanent exhibitions honoring L. C. Anderson High, the school that for years was East Austin's black high school. At the museum's Genealogy Center, families can trace their history through public databases, books, and seminars. Carver was a botanist and inventor (dubbed the Black Leonardo by *Time* magazine) who taught for 47 years at the Tuskegee Institute in Alabama.

Leave the museum and turn right onto Comal Street, which you follow to East 12th Street. On the right at the corner take a moment to look at the ❾ Southgate-Lewis House, home of the W. H. Passon Historical Society. The garden is filled with busts and sculptures of important African American citizens. Wesley H. Passon was a teacher during the late 1800s and early 1900s, and this collection contains two journals in which he recorded the daily affairs of the schools where he served as principal. The house was given to the society in 1986 by a Dr. Albrecht. Turn right onto East 12th Street, pass the handsome Simpson United Methodist Church, and come to the junction with Chicon Street. This was once a dangerous spot, but new bars and restaurants, along with new homes, have ushered in a change of tone.

Keep going past Marshall's Barber Shop and cross the street to ❿ Sam's BBQ, where you should sample a plate of brisket and sausage, whether you are hungry or not. Owner Brian Mays has been serving the East Austin community for decades, and for now keeps turning down the millions of dollars developers offer him for his historic piece of the city. You need only bring him $15 for two meats and two sides, and an extra dollar for the soda machine.

From Sam's, we have the longest leg of the walk. Go back to Chicon and turn left (south). If you are ever driving through this neighborhood, Chicon is the best north–south route. Walk four blocks and turn right on Rosewood Avenue. Walk five blocks to Angelina Street, along which there are several stores you may wish to investigate. If the Swamp Daddy's Ragin Ka-jun trailer at the Ideal Soul Mart is open, order a crawfish po'boy, and for the full experience, eat it inside the store. For more barbecue, walk past Angelina to find Micklethwait Craft Meats, on the south side of Rosewood, which some people say is even better than Franklin.

The last two stops widen the historical focus. Go south one block on Angelina, and turn right on East 11th. Cross the street to enter the ⓫ Texas State Cemetery, where any Texan of note is buried, along with 2,000 Confederate veterans. Established in 1851, it was extensively refurbished in the mid-1990s thanks to legendary Texan and Democrat Lieutenant Governor Bob Bullock, who is of course buried here. Take as much time as you need to study the many fascinating gravestones, but save a few minutes for the exhibits in the visitor center.

Leave the cemetery by the western exit, go left (south) on Navasota Street, and then turn right onto East Ninth Street. Turn left on Lydia Street and then right on East Eighth Street, and go two blocks to San Marcos Street, where you will find the ⓬ French Legation Museum, a white mansion with a wide veranda and some outbuildings inside neat stone walls. Currently the museum is closed for restoration, but the house and grounds are worth inspecting from the street. In 1841 the French government recognized the new Republic of Texas, and one Alphonse Dubois was promoted to chargé d'affaires. He established a legation and commissioned this beautiful house, but as soon as it was completed Sam Houston, furious at President Mirabeau Lamar's decision to establish the capital in this remote and dangerous wilderness, wrested the seat of government to Houston. It wasn't until 1845 that Congress reconvened in Austin and officially settled the matter, at the same session where they agreed to join the United States. A Dr. Joseph W. Robertson took ownership of the property in 1848, and his daughter began giving public tours. When she died, it was looked after by the Daughters of the Republic of Texas. In 2017 the house was taken over by the Texas Historical Commission, which in the process of restoring it.

Follow San Marcos Street north to East 11th to come back to the beginning of the walk.

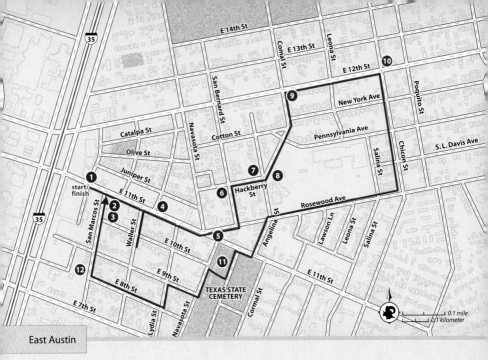

Points of Interest

1 Franklin Barbecue 900 E. 11th St., 512-653-1187, franklinbbq.com

2 Texas Music Museum 1009 E. 11th St., 512-203-4875, texasmusicmuseum.org

3 Ebenezer (Third) Baptist Church 1010 E. 10th St., 512-478-1875, ebc3austin.org

4 Former site of Victory Grill 1104 E. 11th St.

5 Rosewood 1209 Rosewood Ave., 512-838-6205, rosewoodatx.com

6 Wesley United Methodist Church 1164 San Bernard St., 512-478-7007, wesleyunited.org

7 Church of God in Christ #1 1168 Angelina St., 512-478-9261

8 George Washington Carver Museum 1165 Angelina St., 512-974-4926, austintexas.gov/department/george-washington-carver-museum-and-cultural-center

9 Southgate-Lewis House (home of the W. H. Passon Historical Society), 1501 E. 12th St., 512-220-1157

10 Sam's BBQ 2000 E. 12th St., 512-478-0378, samsbarbque.com

11 Texas State Cemetery 909 Navasota St., 512-463-0605, cemetery.tspb.texas.gov

12 French Legation Museum 802 San Marcos St., 512-472-8180, thc.texas.gov/historic-sites/french-legation-state-historic-site

14 East Sixth Street
Cocktails and Community

Above: The migas at Cisco's are not to be missed.

BOUNDARIES: Medina St., Chalmers St., E. Fourth St., E. Sixth St.
DISTANCE: 0.8 mile
DIFFICULTY: Easy
PARKING: Paid street parking on E. Sixth St. and side streets
PUBLIC TRANSIT: Bus 4 to stop 929

East Sixth Street has long passed peak Pabst, but you can still taste the metallic tang of the late 2000s and early 2010s, even if the hipsters' beards are turning gray and their jeans are now slacker. In other words, another generation has grown up, and this slice of Austin has avoided *Portlandia* and ended up another vibrant modern neighborhood that welcomes a new apartment building and a new restaurant almost every week. On this walk we will explore the thriving bar culture of East Sixth and order up some culinary adventures on the side.

Walk Description

Since a certain amount of stamina is required for a night of bar-hopping, we will start with a class at ❶ **Practice Yoga**, a popular studio that is one of the places where Austin does cross over into *Portlandia*-style hippiedom. Embrace the om in the beautifully decorated studio as one of the knowledgeable and enthusiastic instructors leads you through what can be a fairly energetic sequence. Each teacher has a unique style and focus, but all are highly qualified. On Friday nights the studio hosts something different, when Austin's only regular group of Contact Improv practitioners meets. If you have never tried this mashup between dance and martial arts moves, this mixed-level group always welcomes beginners.

Now you have earned a drink, and while we retain some discernment, let's cross the street and enter Austin's best bar, ❷ **Ah Sing Den.** Everything about this place is classy and welcoming. The concept is Victorian opium den, and the decor (vintage couches and chinoiserie) and ambience (somehow smoky without any smoke) successfully take you back to another time. The Asian appetizer-style food serves mainly as an accompaniment to the marvelous cocktails. The Jolly Green Chile, with chile vodka and ginger syrup, is just one standout on the eclectic and inviting menu. They also serve rare Asian spirits—*shochu* and *baijiu*—and Japanese whiskey.

Head east for a block. Our next stop may or may not be open, and you will need to make a reservation. Austin is experiencing a little boom of "secret" bars, and you can find one of these, the ❸ **Milonga Room**, below the Buenos Aires Café at Waller Street. It's a dark 1920s-style cocktail bar serving South American liquors in a room that feels lost in time. Call ahead to make your reservation and get the password. To enter, walk behind the café and ring the bell on the red door.

Time to get a bite of food in your stomach before the next round. Go back to East Sixth Street, and in this same block look for a trailer park on the south side of the street. Here you will find ❹ **Artessano**, a Colombian food trailer serving scrumptious stuffed arepas (and *cazuelas* and South American–style savory empanadas), just the thing to fortify the stomach for more alcohol. Add a delicious *jugo de maracuyá, mora,* or Colombiana soda, and groove to the *vallenato* and reggaeton music for the full Colombian experience.

Walk east one block and turn right on Navasota Street. Cross the light-rail line, and turn right on East Fourth Street to come to the historic ❺ **Scoot Inn**. The oldest continuously running beer joint in Central Texas, it carried on quietly for years in what was a forgotten corner of the city, gradually becoming colonized during the 2000s with the gentrification of East Austin. The inside has recently been remodeled to have more of a lounge-type atmosphere—with a piano player, no less—and the indoor stage has gone, but the large outdoor venue has scratched a permanent entry in the record of the Austin music scene, playing host to a large selection of punk, funk, and rock music that always seems to get everyone dancing. Check the calendar, because if there's a popular band playing, there will be a long line to get in. The Scoot Inn opened in 1871 and somehow stayed open through Prohibition. "Scoot" Ivy and his friend Red bought it in 1955, changing the name to Red's Scoot Inn. They ran the bar until both were in their 70s. The railroad came to Austin in 1871, and the last spike was driven with great fanfare on Christmas Day. Thirsty railroad workers were a big factor in the Scoot Inn's longevity, and the down-at-the-heels buildings to the west on the same block are in fact the last warehouses standing from the railroad's original 1871 plat map. They were bought by Texaco in 1912, were used as an oil depot for many years, and are now used by local artists.

Walk back to East Sixth. One block farther east at Onion Street, climb the steps into ❻ The Brixton. No longer a total dive bar, it has retained its Clash-themed punk rock heart. They have a jukebox full of punk and Motown, bingo every Monday night, a drink called Teaches of Peaches, and annual Misfits karaoke! What more could you want from your drinking environment?

Cross Onion Street to get to the ❼ Hotel Vegas, which is not a hotel and has no connection to Vegas. Instead, this no-frills bar is one of Austin's best punkier venues and the current repository for the noisier and less commercial stream of Austin's constant firehouse of music. Enjoy local shows on the front-room stage with its desert mural, and touring bands like Oh Sees playing out back in

Ah Sing Den on East Sixth Street

the garden. In between the two, there is pool and hip-hop. If you hung out at Emo's during the '90s, this will seem very familiar. The music in the front room is always very loud, says this old man, so take earplugs if you value your hearing, or head next door to sister bar the Volstead Lounge.

Next door to Hotel Vegas is **8** **La Perla**, a tiny cantina with piñatas, norteño music, and a pool table. It's one of the last bastions of Mexican culture on this stretch of East Sixth, so have a beer here while you can. A block south on the west side of Comal Street is **9** **The White Horse**, East Austin's honky-tonking, whiskey-slinging saloon, with happy hour "errrr dam day" from 3 p.m. to 8 p.m. At the far end of the long bar is the dance floor, ready for the big draw: free dance lessons Tuesday–Saturday at 7 p.m., followed by live music so you can show off your new moves. There's blues on Tuesday, swing on Wednesday, and two-step Thursday–Saturday. Any extended stay in the Lone Star State is going to involve two-stepping, so get yourself down to The White Horse and get up to speed on your Texas social skills. It's a fine way to meet people and have a (whiskey) barrel of fun. A side note: if La Matta across Comal is open, order a #3 from this justly lauded and just-opened Italian sandwich shop.

Walk back to Sixth and Comal, and go back in time at **10** **Cisco's**, which is keeping up with the times with a new coat of blue paint and excellent exterior murals. The painting on the east wall features naked women dancing in front of a river. Happily the restaurant is now open until 10 p.m. for dinner. The diner-style interior still has mismatched chairs and an open kitchen area, and the chips come with hot chunky salsa. Their migas are an instant pick-me-up, hangover cure, and all-around panacea and comes with a sausage patty on top. The legendary establishment was opened in 1950 by Rudy "Cisco" Cisneros and is now run by a group that includes his grandson. While we are at this junction, let's give a mention to the new Ramen Tatsu-ya across the street. The chain does serve Austin's best ramen, but you need to go to the north location to experience their top form—somehow the original kitchen kicks slightly harder.

Our last stop is another long-running East Austin favorite. Grackles are some of Austinites' favorite things about Austin, and so is **11** **The Grackle**. Walk east one block to this pub at the northeast corner of the intersection with Chalmers Street along a stretch of East Sixth that bears no relation to the Austin of old. This narrow strip of street is almost always in the shadow of the apartment buildings that tower over both sides, and the experience is more akin to Seattle or Frankfurt than the Austin of only a decade ago. The old-school single-story Grackle is a gem of a bar—not too dilapidated but with no airs and a friendly staff, and it has a Pac-Man table and dartboards. Happy hour is from 6 p.m. to 8 p.m. every day, and there are often DJ's and always a great food truck (or two). They carry an extensive and excellent whiskey selection, and although they do not have Laphroaig, the Port Charlotte is an excellent substitute.

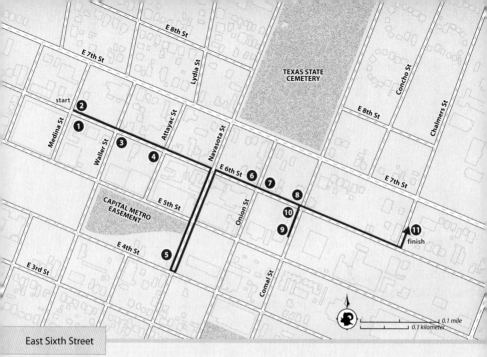

East Sixth Street

Points of Interest

1 Practice Yoga 1103 E. Sixth St., 512-730-1638, practiceyogaaustin.com

2 Ah Sing Den 1100 E. Sixth St., 512-467-4280, ahsingden.com

3 Milonga Room 1201 E. Sixth St., 512-382-1189, buenosairescafe.com/milonga-room

4 Artessano 1211 E. Sixth St., 512-387-5353

5 Scoot Inn 1308 E. Fourth St., scootinnaustin.com

6 The Brixton 1412 E. Sixth St., 512-370-2749, thebrixtonaustin.com

7 Hotel Vegas 1502 E. Sixth St., texashotelvegas.com

8 La Perla 1512 E. Sixth St., 512-477-0167

9 The White Horse 500 Comal St., 512-553-6756, thewhitehorseaustin.com

10 Cisco's 1511 E. Sixth Street, 512-478-2420, ciscosaustin.com

11 The Grackle 1700 E. Sixth St., 512-520-8148

15 Goat Cave Karst Nature Preserve
Underground Secrets

Above: A cave entrance, portal to an underground world

DISTANCE: 0.8 mile
DIFFICULTY: Moderate
PARKING: Rough parking on the lot next door (to the east) or street parking on Coastal Dr.
PUBLIC TRANSIT: Bus 333 to stop 3216

Karst is the name for the terrain from the Colorado River to the Pecos River that comprises 20% of Texas. It's the reason Austin has Barton Springs and San Antonio had Pearl Beer. Briefly, 100 million years ago Central Texas was at the bottom of an ocean, and the skeletons of trillions of shellfish were slowly compressed into layers of solid limestone. Eventually the waters receded for good, and 15 million years ago the same chain of tectonic shifts that lifted up the Rockies cracked and fractured the rock layers from Dallas to Del Rio, along what is called the Balcones Fault. This fault line is the edge of Texas's Hill Country and is the geological dividing line between the American West and the South. Limestone is calcium carbonate, and when exposed to rainwater—which is in fact a weak carbonic acid because of the dissolved carbon dioxide—the carbonate reacts to form soluble calcium bicarbonate. Water drips or floods into fissures and clefts and over time carves channels through the rock. Most of these are finger-sized, but some of them have become vast caverns. In totality they make up the huge underground reservoir called the Edwards Aquifer. San Antonio and much of the Hill Country depend on the aquifer for water, which recharges slowly through a narrow strip of land along the Balcones Fault. This is why so many Central Texans fight constantly to protect the aquifer from development and overpumping, and why limiting impervious cover in the recharge area is crucial to the region's growth and sustainability.

You can descend into the underground world at places like Longhorn Cavern and Natural Bridge Caverns, but most of the thousands of caves in the Hill Country are hard to find and difficult and dangerous to access. They are also home to many strange species, collectively known as troglobites—cave spiders, millipedes, isopods, and blind salamanders. Some of these animals were sea creatures who managed to adapt when the water dried up. Bats live down there too; the world's largest colony is at Bracken Cave, north of San Antonio. At Goat Cave Karst Nature Preserve you can't go underground, but you can see the entrances to three wet caves. The preserve is a narrow 8-acre strip along Coastal Drive between Davis Lane and Alexandria Drive, an area that is in transition. At the eastern end of Davis Lane, the street is a leafy two-lane throwback through old South Austin, but on the western side of Brodie, more recent urban spread is visible: newer subdivisions and apartments line a four-lane divided highway. Let's thank the City of Austin for preserving this sliver of Hill Country terrain.

Walk Description

Access to ❶ **Goat Cave Karst Nature Preserve** is from the sidewalk through wooden railings just west of the sign that is visible from Davis Lane. Not all that long ago, this was the Wade ranch, but nature has reclaimed the park and covered it with the flora typical of the Hill Country. The rocky surface is dimpled with hollows; the stone Swiss cheese is the result of the chemical reaction described above. The main path finds its way along the center of the preserve, stopping at a rainwater-retention pond close to the end of Coastal Avenue. It's narrow and rough, even though the terrain is perfectly level. Vegetation crowds the passage, and I would recommend long pants even though this is a short walk. The woods are also home to raccoons and foxes, and you might see a deer. Austin's wildernesses, however compact, retain their wildness. Because this is primarily a nature preserve, no pets are allowed. The first of the path section is bordered with limestone blocks. Almost immediately you will find the first cave, Wade Cave, in a small clearing with a bench, to the left of the trail. The round cave opening has what might be steps going down into it, possibly from earlier explorations, though a metal fence sensibly deters investigations. A sign explains how water carries everything in its path into the cave, through the aquifer, and out into Barton Springs. A little farther is a larger information sign with a trail map, information on the park's fauna, and another diagram of how the Edwards Aquifer works. The layer of water-bearing karst varies from 300 to 700 feet in thickness and holds somewhere between 25 and 55 million acre-feet (a lot), though only about 5% of that is available for extraction. The eight counties in the San Antonio metropolitan area, which keeps growing, pump more than 200 million gallons of water from the aquifer every day.

Beyond the sign, the trail goes down a few widely spaced steps to reach Hideout Cave on your left. It's another small hole going down into the darkness, as if someone had cut a hole in a piecrust. The sign here shows pictures of some of the strange animals that live down in the damp darkness, like the pseudoscorpion and harvester spiders. Aboveground, birds chirp in the bushes. Dense green underbrush and tall elms and oaks alternate with cedar forest and grassy clearings dotted with mesquite, in the typical Hill Country mix of vegetation. As always in karst terrain, the rocky paths require your attention while walking.

At a Y junction where there is a simple bench, turn left to face Goat Cave. The entrance is behind a tall chain-link fence, so you cannot get very close, for your protection and that of the bats that live there. A sign shows an article from the September 1957 edition of the *Austin American-Statesman* that tells how the cave got its name. Spoiler alert: some men found a goat who had fallen in, though the story has a twist that you will read about when you get there.

From Goat Cave the trail more or less follows an old ranch fence until it emerges into the open space that contains the retention pond. You could either turn left to reach Coastal Drive and walk back along the street or simply retrace your steps. Goat Cave Karst Nature Preserve may be small, but the short walk through this space provides a blast of the outside, a glimpse into the land's recent ranching past, and a deeper understanding of the natural systems that are just beneath the streets.

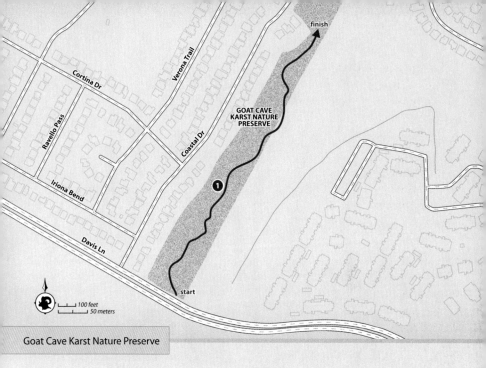

Goat Cave Karst Nature Preserve

Point of Interest

1 Goat Cave Karst Nature Preserve 3900 Deer Run (access is from Davis Lane)

16 Hornsby Bend
Colorado Bottomlands

Above: Wildlife at Hornsby Bend

BOUNDARIES: Colorado River, Farm to Market Road 973
DISTANCE: 4.3 miles
DIFFICULTY: Easy
PARKING: On-site at the treatment ponds
PUBLIC TRANSIT: None

On the other bank of the river from the still-unreconstructed neighborhood of Del Valle, tucked into the eponymous bend, is Austin's most unusual nature reserve, on the grounds of the Hornsby Bend Biosolids Management Plant. This plant consists of a series of vast ponds and some hayfields surrounding huge piles of, well, let's say that this is where the city turns nutrient-rich sewage sludge and yard trimmings into its famous Dillo Dirt compost. The raw sewage is treated in several large ponds, and the water then goes to irrigate the hayfields. (Old Reuben

Hornsby would be impressed. See Backstory, page 93.) These ponds attract large numbers of waterfowl, and the birds in turn attract many avian enthusiasts to the facility. Austin Water established the ❶ Center for Environmental Research at Hornsby Bend "for research and education about ecology and urban sustainability," and the center worked with the birding community to set up the Hornsby Bend Bird Observatory. It also set about repairing the site's 3.5 miles of riverside, and along with the observatory, this restored habitat is what we will explore.

Walk Description

To get to the parking area, use the main entrance on Farm to Market Road 973 and, once past the security booth, drive between the facility offices and one of the hayfields. Look for the sign pointing up a ramp that says GENERAL PUBLIC. This leads past a hedge to the raised ponds, an impressive and unexpected sight on first viewing. Ahead of you, the tallest buildings of downtown are visible on the horizon. To your right is the extensive Dillo Dirt operation, and to your left, the woods along the river. Make a sharp left as soon as you pass the hedge, and drive carefully past Pond 1 and Pond 2 to the southeast corner of this area. Park at the corner on the grass beside the road.

Long grasses flutter on either side of the narrow track, and duck trails ruffle the pond surfaces. A wide grass path leads down from this spot into the woods. This is the River Trail, our route for today. It follows the curve of the Colorado 3 miles to Platt Lane, at the north end of the facility (we are not going that far). Walk by a yellow metal gate to enter the trail, clearly an old ranch track. The path is surrounded by lush greenery, and on my last visit muscadine vines covered much of the trees and bushes. Deer leapt up out of the tall grasses, and spiny orb weavers lay in wait at the center of their large webs. (This is a good time to remind you to wear long pants, preferably soaked in permethrin, anytime you go into long grass, as a protection against ticks.)

Soon the path makes a right to align with the river, though the wide expanse of amber water is obscured by the woods that surround the trail. To see it clearly turn left down the Lower Island View Trail when you see a yellow control valve to the right. This path takes you over sandy soil through the hackberry-forested bottomland to the mighty Colorado, whose shades of brown and green echo the colors of the wooded shores. To your right is the island for which the trail is named. These islands along the Colorado are formed by sediment carried by the stream.

Retrace your steps to the main trail and turn left to soon arrive at another junction. Remember this junction, as we will turn left here on the return trip to visit the bird observatory on Pond 2. The Upper Island View Trail to the left is similar to the Lower but with palmettos. The map shows that this trail is a loop that connects back to the main trail; however, that has not been my experience. If you take this diversion, come back from the river the way you came. Continue through the woods and look for an ancient pecan tree, a few yards from the path on your right. Climb a slight incline where a metal building comes into sight. This is the Aquatic Greenhouse, a very, very long shed containing two rectangular ponds that run the length of the structure. Take a peek inside. The lengths of metal tracery holding up the roof make neat geometric patterns as they converge on the far wall.

The path, now concrete, follows the side of the greenhouse. At the end of the building, the service road to the right leads up to Pond 2, and a track to the left goes down into the riverside forest. The trail goes straight ahead up a small incline to the berm that forms the southwestern edge of Pond 3. This pond is very different from the others, which are flat expanses of water tousled by birds and breezes. Pond 3 is an almost empty lake, dotted with dead trees and enclosed by a narrow strip of tangled branches through which you can see the bright-green algae covering the water surface. Birds chirp from the impenetrable thickets. The trail follows the bank, heading north-northeast for a while under a tunnel of leaves and branches. Catch sight of the river glistening through the woods to your left. Jets roar low overhead as they approach the airport. Depending on the wind direction, you might encounter the plant's signature aroma wafting from the piles of Dillo Dirt.

The track curves slightly right as it approaches the end of the ponds and comes to a T at an access road. In front of you is a huge pylon and a small shed. Turn right along the road, passing some pipes on the left, and keep an eye out for the trail sign pointing left. Follow it, walking off the road and through a dip that has become a sort of graveyard for rusting tanks and other equipment.

This section of the trail is very different, passing through a familiar Hill Country environment of pretty savanna dotted with honey mesquite trees. In spring these old meadows are a riot of wildflowers and butterflies. The trail turns right at a thick hedge, from which deer might leap out as you pass, then goes left along a ranch track, crossing the hedgeline into what must have been a separate field. Maybe Reuben Hornsby himself laid out these bygone fields. Thistles, cactus, and even lavender cover the ground. Watch for a left turn where the trail leaves the jeep track (which continues straight and can easily be mistaken for the correct route) to go back to following the curve of the river.

You will arrive at a Y junction, where a short spur goes down to the river. This patch of riverbank has some history, along with a multitude of what look like flood-measuring devices. A sign tells the story of the old Hergotz Crossing. On the other side of the river a wooded bank rises to what was known as Hergotz Hill, now part of Johnson's Backyard Garden at the end of Hergotz Lane. According to the sign, the hill was used as a refuge in the 1800s when the Colorado flooded.

Backstory: Reuben Hornsby

Hornsby Bend is named for Travis County's first settler, Reuben Hornsby, a surveyor with Stephen F. Austin, who was granted 4,600 acres in this bend on the Colorado in 1832. This settlement formed the basis for the establishment of Austin in 1839 and Travis County in 1840 (previously Bastrop was the largest nearby center of population). Hornsby was William Barton's nearest neighbor when Barton moved from Bastrop (to get away from his neighbors) to live by Barton Creek on the other side of Austin (for more on William Barton, see page 25). J. W. Wilbarger wrote of Hornsby's land: "Washed on the west by the Colorado, it stretches over a level valley about three miles wide to the east . . . covered with wild rye, and looking like one vast green wheat field." The writer must have had an interesting visit because, according to a stone marking Hornsby's homesite, Wilbarger spent some period of 1833 recovering from a scalping. According to Wilbarger, Austin and others rode up the Colorado from Bastrop looking for places to settle, and Hornsby was the last to be satisfied. But when they saw the bend in the river, he was at last happy. "Laying down his gun Hornsby turned to his friends. 'Boys, this suits me just fine,' he said. 'You can go on home if you like.' " A true pioneer, he brought cattle to the area and registered the first brand in Travis County. He helped Edwin Waller lay out the new city and died after a lifetime of service in 1879, at age 86.

But Westerners had come to this spot much earlier than that. In 1709 two priests, Isidro Félix de Espinosa and Antonio de San Buenaventura y Olivares, accompanied by Captain Pedro de Aguirre, mounted an expedition from San Juan Bautista presidio on the Rio Grande (now Guerrero, Coahuila). Espinosa and Olivares hoped to convert the Tejas Indians, while the official goal was to dissuade them from trading with the French in Louisiana. They pushed past San Antonio to the Colorado and camped on Hergotz Hill while they explored the river valley, and it's likely they crossed the river at this point. Although the men were impressed by the rich lands they discovered, the expedition found the tribes unwelcoming, and as a result the Spanish held off on their mission-building activities in Texas.

The Hergotz crossing is a good place to turn around. The trail does go on to Pratt Lane, climbing away from the river through a mix of deciduous and juniper woodland, but there are no more surprises, and the rest of our time is better spent at the bird shelter. Retrace your winding steps through the fields and past Pond 3 and the greenhouse, back into the bottomland woods. Turn left at the junction, and walk up the slope to the bank of Pond 2, where you will find the ❷ Hornsby Bend Bird Observatory, built in 1999 and designed for unobstructed views and to be completely off-grid. This was the same year that developers demolished the iconic Liberty Lunch venue downtown (page 16), and because in Austin everything is connected to music,

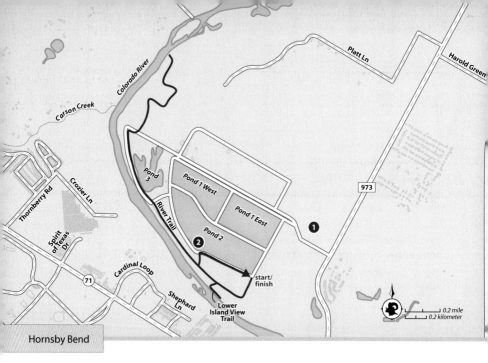

Hornsby Bend

this shelter was constructed from materials salvaged from the demolition. Birders first began visiting the "Platt" ponds in 1959, after they were discovered by G. Frank "Pancho" Oatman, who noticed ducks flying across the river while he was visiting his family in Del Valle. The list of birds you can see here is extensive and varies from month to month, and the best way to begin would be to join one of the monthly birding field trips that take place on the third Saturday of each month, on which you are guaranteed to see at least 50 species. Or you can simply spend a few moments enjoying the peaceful breezes while you watch avian comings and goings at Austin's most unusual natural resource.

Points of Interest

1 Austin Water Center for Environmental Research 2210 FM 973, 512-972-1960

2 Hornsby Bend Bird Observatory 2210 FM 973, hornsbybend.org

17 Hyde Park
Austin's First Suburb

Above: Colonel Monroe Shipe's house

BOUNDARIES: Ave. B, 45th St., Duval St., W. 39th St.
DISTANCE: 2.9 miles
DIFFICULTY: Easy
PARKING: Street parking on Avenue B in front of the AISD Baker Building
PUBLIC TRANSIT: Buses 1 and 801 to stop 606

Hyde Park was constructed in the 1890s by the Missouri, Kansas and Texas Land and Town Co., who with typical Texas swagger named it after London's poshest neighborhood. It was Austin's first suburb and contains some of the city's oldest and most historic homes. The company envisioned it as an affluent place full of large, comfortable houses. To promote the development, Colonel Monroe Shipe, the agent, built parks, a pavilion, and even a streetcar line for quick access to downtown. But sales were slow, and Shipe switched tactics to target middle- and lower-income buyers, so overall the neighborhood has a preponderance of bungalows, most of which were built between 1924 and 1935. The neighborhood has for a while been one of Austin's quiet attractions, but the turn to preservation was gradual and followed a long period of decline. It took a lot of hard work and perseverance from owners to restore their homes to the excellent condition you see now.

You will find an eclectic mix of building styles, from late 19th-century Queen Anne and Classical Revival homes to 20th-century bungalows and ranch houses. The leafy streets are full of plaques, as 44 structures (41 houses, one commercial building, the Elisabet Ney Museum, and the Fire Station) are designated as City of Austin Historic Landmarks. Many of these have been added to the National Register of Historic Places and the list of Texas Historic Landmarks, and most are in the Hyde Park Historic District, registered in 1990, which comprises the blocks between 40th and 45th Streets, and Avenue A and Duval Street.

Walk Description

Begin on the 3900 block of Avenue B, just outside the Historic District, for a look at the old **❶ Baker School** on the western side of the street. This handsome building was indeed once a school and was built on the site of Monroe Shipe's pavilion. Austin Independent School District (AISD) had used it as a professional development center but recently sold it to the owners of the Alamo Theater chain, who plan to use the building as their corporate headquarters.

At the corner of Avenue B and 40th Street is **❷ Hyde Park Presbyterian Church.** This church was built in 1896 by the Hyde Park Baptists, whose Reverend Beverly modeled the design on the neighborhood pavilion. In 1909 it was moved to 406 W. 40th St., and the Baptists shared it with the Presbyterians until the Baptists moved to a newer, bigger building in 1911. The Presbyterians moved this church to its current address in 1921. The white-painted clapboard church with its small tower is one of the few nonresidential historic buildings in Hyde Park.

Turn right (east) on 40th Street. The first building on the south side of the street past Avenue C is the **❸ Smith-Marcuse-Lowry House,** a National Register property that was one of the first to be built in the neighborhood. The two-story house is an excellent example of the Queen Anne style, with eclectic ornamentation typical of the Victorian era, including the polygonal tower on the north elevation. It's a great example of the kind of large house that the Missouri, Kansas and Texas Land and Town Co. encouraged owners to build, hoping to attract potential customers.

Keep going on 40th Street and turn left on Speedway, the neighborhood's main north–south street and the Continental Divide between east and west addresses. Finally you have crossed into the Hyde Park Historic District. Shipe's wide avenues were planted with a variety of shade trees, and to walk along these streets is to walk through a forest with houses. The soft sound of doves fills the air, and you may notice the scent of magnolia flowers. Pass the ❹ **Robert T. Badger House** at 4006 Speedway, admiring the classical columns and handsome verandas. At 41st and Speedway is a ❺ **Moonlight Tower,** one of 15 that the city erected to illuminate the streets in the late 1890s and refurbished in the 1990s. Turn left onto 41st and at 213 W. 41st St. pass the large ❻ **Curl-Crockett House,** with porches that wrap around two sides of the main building. The modest ❼ **Schenken-Oatman House** at 311 W. 41st St. is a charming example of the bungalows that appealed to the lower-income buyers of the time.

Go right at the small roundabout at Avenue B. The next building to look for is the ❽ **Elvira T. Manor Davis House,** the last house on the left before 42nd Street. Mrs. Davis had the house built when she was widowed (her husband was a quarryman who supplied stone for the Capitol) and lived here until 1918. The columns and bay window lean toward the Classical Revival style.

Keep north three blocks until you get to the corner of West 45th Street, where you will find the Queen Anne–style ❾ **F. T. and Belle Ramsey House.** Built in 1894 for horticulturist F. T. Ramsey, the building remains noteworthy, with its steep-pitched roof, two-story porches, and jigsaw trim, despite being half-hidden by vegetation and having a general air of needing some TLC.

Turn around and look for the ❿ **Avenue B Grocery & Market** on the left at number 4403. Austin's oldest continuously operated grocery was built in 1909 and has a simple square wooden facade hiding a pitched roof. It is justly renowned for its sandwiches—I recommend a King Combo of roast beef, ham, turkey, and three cheeses or the vegetarian Queen B, taken with a soda and a break at one of the benches beside the store.

Turn left out of the store and then left onto West 43rd Street at another roundabout. In the second block you will pass the ⓫ **Clark-Emmert House** at 4300 Ave. D, a beautiful, larger single-story home with an ornate front porch. Gustav and Anna Emmert were German immigrants. Their daughter Violet, who died in 2004 at the age of 101, was a secretary to Texas governors Ma and Pa Ferguson.

Just across Speedway on East 43rd is ⓬ **Austin Fire Department Station 9,** which the city has repeatedly recommended be closed since 1971, only to be rebuffed by Hyde Park residents. The half-timbered building has a Germanic look. On the eastern side of the alley across the street at 4212 Ave. F is the beautifully restored ⓭ **Kopperl House.**

Keep going east and turn left on Avenue F, coming to the much-missed ⓮ **Shipe Neighborhood Park** and Shipe Pool, which unfortunately was closed for renovations at press time. The wooden bathrooms just outside the pool area are a small architectural delight.

The grounds of the ⓯ Elizabet Ney Museum take up the whole block east of Shipe and straddle Waller Creek. German immigrant Ney was a famous sculptor who came to Austin in 1882. She was a star recruit to the new neighborhood and built the castlelike limestone studio she called Formosa. "Wildly iconoclastic" and "one of a kind" is how she was described, and the museum exuberantly celebrates her life and art. Much of the lot is left as unkempt wildlife habitat, and works by contemporary artists often add interest to the grounds.

Cross Waller Creek over a little dam at the back of the museum, and walk across the grass to East 45th Street. At Duval, this walk's eastern boundary, you might choose to cross 45th Street to visit Juiceland and Exploded Records, icons of contemporary Austin. Continue south on Duval, crossing Waller Creek again on a pretty stone bridge. Look left for a quick view into the slim vein of earth bank and limestone bed. Keep south and arrive at Duval and 43rd, a quintessential Austin intersection that is home to several cherished businesses. How many lives have left traces here, in shared soups and salads at Mother's Cafe, bottomless coffees and cookies at Quack's, and pajama-clad midnight runs to Pronto Food Market? Sadly the new owners of this convenience store removed the poem by Bard of Hyde Park Albert Huffstickler (who died in 2002) that used to be displayed here in one of his haunts.

If you did not have a sandwich at Avenue B Grocery, you might try the tantalizing food offerings at Asti or Julio's, or the award-winning french fries from Hyde Park Bar & Grill. Take your selfie at the famous fork sign outside that restaurant, then head south and take the next right onto East 42nd Street. Turn left onto Avenue H and look for 4107 on the left, the ⓰ Williams-Weigl House. This spruce-looking Texas Historic Landmark was built by the Williamses around 1911. In 1947 F. Lee Weigl, another German and an ironworker by trade, moved in. His company produced hand-wrought works for the Capitol and the University of Texas, as well as for private homes, and was in business until 1977. (His workshop was at Cesar Chavez and Waller Creek, where the Ironworks BBQ restaurant, page 68, still displays his sign.)

Keep going and take another right and left, onto East 41st and then Avenue G, noting the ⓱ Philquist-Wood House on your left at 4007 E. 41st, another Texas Historic Landmark. Cross East 40th and say farewell to the Hyde Park Historic District.

Arrive at the intersection of East 40th and Avenue G. Even though we have left the historic district, it is the site of three of the loveliest houses in Hyde Park, all on the National Register of Historic Places. At 3913 Ave. G is the perfectly proportioned ⓲ Page-Gilbert House, built in 1893 by Christopher Page, a British immigrant and stonemason who worked on the Texas state Capitol. The demure brick house soft-pedals the Victorian style and, unusually, adds Queen Anne accents like the steeple roof and scalloped shingles. It was the only brick house in Hyde Park at the time, maybe because Page's British bones balked at a house made of wood. What did he think of the ⓳ **Frank M. and Annie G. Covert House** opposite, a massive two-story mansion that was the neighborhood's second brick home? Maybe he convinced the Coverts of the advantages of the material. The L-shaped building, practically unaltered, features an elaborate roofscape and a two-story wraparound porch and, like Page's house, blends Queen Anne elements into a typical Victorian mansion. Note the scalloped shingles, the double columns on the grand porch, and the weathervanes. The Covert name is still well known in Austin, attached to various car dealerships that Frank started. Two doors down is the 1902 ⓴ **Hildreth-Flanagan-Heierman House**. This, another large two-story home, adds Classical Revival touches to Victorian-era features. Note the Doric columns on the two-tier porch. The house is an unusual snapshot of the shift in design from late 19th- to early 20th-century architecture.

Walk down Avenue G to East 39th Street, which is curved because it was part of the racetrack that was on the fairgrounds. At the southwestern corner is the most unusual home of the neighborhood, the ㉑ **Shipe House**. One of the first houses in Hyde Park, this was the dwelling place of Colonel Shipe himself. It was built in 1892, in part with wood from the fairgrounds that the new

The Page-Gilbert House

neighborhood replaced. The ridgeline is oddly low, and Shipe covered the roof in concrete early on, possibly to try and keep the house cool. This was later removed. Three chimneys rise from one corner, another detail that adds to the general "steamboat wheelhouse on acid" appearance. The house was meant to be a showcase for the new neighborhood and amply demonstrates Shipe's eclectic taste with its exotic mix of Eastlake, Stick, and Swiss chalet styles.

Continue along 39th Street. At Avenue F you are confronted with a side of the huge Hyde Park Baptist Church complex. Turn left, and at the next corner is the ㉒ Mansbendel-Williams House, built in 1925. Peter Mansbendel was a talented and successful woodcarver from Basel in Switzerland who married Shipe's daughter, Clotilde, whom Shipe met in New York. The couple lived at Dad's for a while before moving back to New York but came back to Austin in 1915. Their stuccoed and half-timbered house is a classic Tudor Revival–style home and was a labor of love for Mansbendel. He also had a big hand in the single-story ㉓ William T. and Valerie Mansbendel Williams House next door at 3820 Ave. F, built in 1933 for Mansbendel's daughter Valerie and her husband. This house, also in the Tudor Revival style, has hardly changed since its construction. Both houses are on the National Register.

Walk back to East 39th Street and turn left to walk the four blocks back to the start, pausing to take in the ㉔ Sears-King House, a Queen Anne–style house at 209 W. 39th St., unchanged since it was built in 1903.

Points of Interest

1 Former site of the Baker School 3908 Ave. B

2 Hyde Park Presbyterian Church 3913 Ave. B, 512-459-7747, hydeparkaustin.org

3 Smith-Marcuse-Lowry House 3913 Ave. C

4 Robert T. Badger House 4006 Speedway

5 Moonlight Tower W. 41st St. and Speedway

6 Curl-Crockett House 213 W. 41st St.

7 Schenken-Oatman House 311 W. 41st St.

8 Elvira T. Manor Davis House 4112 Ave. B

9 F. T. and Belle Ramsey House 4412 Ave. B

10 Ave. B Grocery & Market 4403 Ave. B, 512-453-3921, avenuebgrocery.com

11 Clark-Emmert House 4300 Ave. D

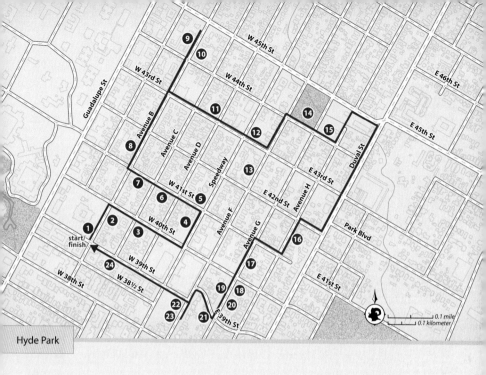

Hyde Park

12 Austin Fire Department Station 9 4301 Speedway

13 Kopperl House 4212 Ave. F

14 Shipe Neighborhood Park 4400 Ave. G, shipepark.org

15 Elizabet Ney Museum 304 E. 44th St., 512-974-1625, austintexas.gov/elisabetney

16 Williams-Weigl House 4107 Ave. H

17 Philquist-Wood House 4007 Ave. G

18 Page-Gilbert House 3913 Ave. G

19 Frank M. and Annie G. Covert House 3912 Ave. G

20 Hildreth-Flanagan-Heierman House 3909 Ave. G

21 Shipe House 3816 Ave. G

22 Mansbendel-Williams House 3824 Ave. F

23 William T. and Valerie Mansbendel Williams House 3820 Ave. F

24 Sears-King House 209 W. 39th St.

18 Inga's Trail at Bull Creek Greenbelt
In Comanche Territory

BOUNDARIES: Bull Creek District Park and Spicewood Springs Road
DISTANCE: 3.4 miles
DIFFICULTY: Difficult, for water crossings and rough patches, though the trail is mostly level
PARKING: At Bull Creek District Park; at the access point on Lakewood Drive; or at the north end on Old Spicewood Springs Drive
PUBLIC TRANSIT: None

Together with Onion and Walnut Creeks, Bull Creek is one of the three streams that very roughly define Austin's erstwhile outer limits, though development has long pushed the metro area beyond all three. Its source is close to Ranch to Market Road 2222 and RM 620, and the main branch joins with two other tributaries just west of Spicewood Springs Road. That road follows the creek to its junction with Loop 360, where two more branches augment the flow. The channel winds down the valley to meet the river just east of the Pennybacker Bridge. The towering

Backstory: Bull Creek

Bull Creek has played its part in Austin's history. In the Shoal Creek walk (page 136), we will meet Janet Long Fish, who in the 1950s reopened a section of the old Comanche Trail along that stream. It seems likely that the original trail of that name continued from Shoal Creek past Mount Bonnell and followed Bull Creek before heading west to Comanche Peak north of Lake Travis. Stephen F. Austin deeded the land to settlers, and among the early inhabitants were Will Preece and his wife. Their two sons both went on to be Texas Rangers who fought against the Comanche. Will's grandson Harold Preece was a writer for the *Austin American-Statesman* specializing in Americana and was an early supporter of civil rights. According to an article he wrote about his grandfather, "the stream came to be called Bull Creek after Will Preece killed a buffalo that he spotted drinking in its channel." Preece goes on to say that "a few miles from the Preece ranch lay the southern terminus of the bloody Comanche Trail with its northern end being seven hundred miles away in Western Kansas." Because the southern end of the Comanche Trail is considered to have been across the Rio Grande in Mexico, he must have been confused or exaggerating. The Preeces and their neighbors soon had the area tamed, since in 1846 the Mormons, who by then had established various communities in Travis County, built a road along Bull Creek to a mill on Spicewood Springs Road. This became a scenic drive, and what remains of it is now part of Lakewood Drive. A family called Walden bought land along the creek sometime after 1850, and in the 1900s they began to charge for access to the swimming hole. Eventually the tract was acquired by the city and became a public park. Inga VanNynatten, whose magnetism attracted the volunteer labor that built and maintains the current footpath and for whom it is named, died in 2000 at age 30 of breast cancer.

cliffs and green slopes along the canyon are strikingly picturesque, and this creekside trail grants walkers vistas of some of the city's most dramatic scenery. On this hike you will pass under high bluffs and walk alongside waterfalls tumbling into deep, clear pools. The heat of summer draws a crowd to ❶ **Bull Creek District Park + Greenbelt**, and archaeological investigations show that people have been enjoying this paradise for at least 9,000 years. Be prepared for some rough and possibly muddy terrain; this is a hike, not a walk, and the suggested route has three creek crossings. You should not attempt to cross the creek if the water is high.

Walk Description

This walk begins at Bull Creek District Park. Turn east off Loop 360 at the Lakewood Drive lights, then look for the first left turn into the parking lot. In front of you under a green cliff is a long pool between vertical rock walls. The creek gushes down into the pool from a narrow channel between two limestone shelves. Make your way through brush over the slippery rock shelves on the western side of the stream, and walk under the Loop 360 bridge. You are looking for a small concrete dam just beyond the bridge, where you can cross the creek. Pick up the Inga VanNynatten Memorial Trail on the eastern side of Bull Creek, and head upstream. Thick undergrowth surrounds the narrow, rocky trail. A sign marks a short detour around an eroded section. There are many spurs leading left to the water and right to semiofficial access points, but keep parallel to the creek and you won't go wrong.

After just under 0.5 mile cross a ditch and come to the water's edge. Pause to admire the pretty stream flowing into the creek on the opposite side. Continue past sycamores along a pitted shelf of the whitish limestone typical of the Edwards Plateau. The trail passes some burbling falls then veers back into the woods before coming to a fork. Keep left to come to the walk's main attraction, known as Link Falls. A large rock ledge angles across the creek, creating a waterfall and a long, deep swimming hole. There's even a beach. Tall cliffs tower over the scene, and low bluffs on the other side of the creek are perfect for jumping into the cool water. On a hot day this place will be buzzing, but on any day it is worth a visit for the view up the valley.

Continue to a road that goes over a low water crossing. Inga's Trail continues on the other side of the asphalt and goes under the second set of concrete Loop 360 bridges, where the whir and rumble of traffic echoes in the valley. Just past the bridge look for another small dam where you must ford the creek for the second time. The trail picks up on the left (north) side of the creek on a plateau of grass and cedar coppices. Ahead are the huge bluffs, towering over the valley. Come to a fork where there is a bench. To the left is an alternate route to Old Spicewood Springs Road. Take the less promising-looking overgrown right fork, which takes you to the third creek crossing. Look for a red fire hydrant in the middle of the creek, clearly the answer to a question in an Austin trivia quiz. After the crossing, the trail climbs into a cedar forest. Look for some steps to the left, marked as Inga's Trail, that descend to the confluence mentioned in the introduction. Laurel Oaks Creek enters from the right as Bull Creek makes a sharp turn northwest. This beautiful spot, which is the far point of today's walk, deserves a few moments of exploration. You could also cross the creek and go right a few yards up Old Spicewood Springs Road to investigate the short Irving and Hazeline Smith Memorial Trail.

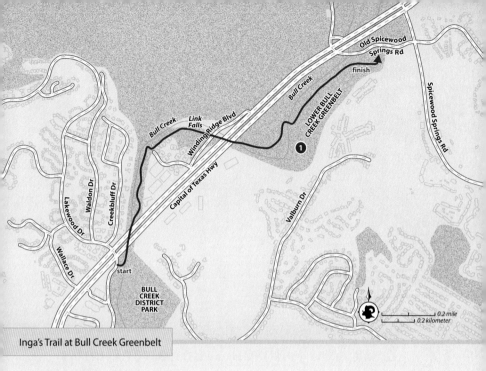

Inga's Trail at Bull Creek Greenbelt

Point of Interest

1 Bull Creek District Park + Greenbelt Access at Bull Creek District Park: 6701 Lakewood Dr.

19 Lady Bird Johnson Wildflower Center
The First Lady's Legacy

Above: *The main entrance of the Wildflower Center*

BOUNDARIES: Mopac Expy. (TX 1), LaCrosse Ave.
DISTANCE: 2.2 miles (to complete all the trails)
DIFFICULTY: Easy
PARKING: At the center and on LaCrosse Ave.
PUBLIC TRANSIT: None

The ❶ Lady Bird Johnson Wildflower Center is a whole lot more than its name implies, though the name is probably better branding than something like the Ecological Research and Design and Plant Conservation Center. Wildflower center experts provided advice after the Blanco River floods of 2016; invented the trademarked SkySystem, a soil made from recycled materials for green roofs; and of course continue to develop ecological roadsides, continuing the work set in motion by Lady Bird Johnson's crowning achievement, the Highway Beautification Act, which

Backstory: Lady Bird Johnson

Her nurse declared that Claudia Alta Taylor, born in Karnack, Texas, in 1912, was "as pretty as a ladybird," and the nickname stuck. The East Texas native graduated from the University of Texas at Austin with a bachelor's degree in art and was studying to be a reporter when she met rising politician Lyndon Johnson. She used her status as first lady to fight for women's rights and was a pioneering environmentalist, advocating for open spaces and greenbelts as an integral part of urbanization. Lady Bird was galvanized by her love of the natural world, and the results of her lifelong work can be seen not just in the roadside wildflower displays that are such a feature of springtime in Texas, but also in city parks all over the country. She planted the seed in Ann Butler's mind for the transformation of the banks of the Colorado in Austin (see "Lady Bird Lake Boardwalks," page 110). Her ideas have gone mainstream in the world of urban planning, and the city has many fine examples (most covered in this book) of green spaces that provide delight and respite for humans, and homes for plants and animals. The wildflower center, which she opened in 1982 and which moved from East Austin to this location in 1995, is a living memorial to this remarkable human being whose ideas are still inspiring people to make the world better.

celebrated its 50th anniversary in 2015. Johnson's best-known quote is rendered in metal at the entrance: "My special cause, the one that alerts my interest and quickens the pace of my life, is to preserve the wildflowers and native plants that define the regions of our land—to encourage and promote their use in appropriate areas, and thus help pass on to generations in waiting the quiet joys and satisfactions I have known since my childhood." The gardens, buildings, and café have a gentle Zen-like charm, and it would be easy to let a couple of hours fly by in quiet appreciation of all that is on offer. But beware: you may find yourself drawn Alice-like down a rabbit hole of enthusiasm for Texas's native plants. On a practical note, bring a hat and sunscreen, especially if you plan to complete the longer hikes, where there is little shade.

Walk Description

The center allows for all levels of interaction. You can pop in to smell the flowers, visit the store, and enjoy a cup of coffee in the café, or you could immerse yourself in guided tours and classes in drawing and botany. The grounds are helpful to those who want to learn more about the native flora, as they are arranged as a series of microenvironments that include savanna, woodland, and a host of tiny examples of different types of gardens. It's a small Disneyland of natural Texas, which we can divide into four areas: the Central Complex, the Central Gardens, the garden trail, and two longer trails of about a mile each that explore the managed areas and wildlands that make up the rest of these 300 or so acres on the plain between Slaughter and Bear Creeks.

From the parking lot you walk up a gravel path to a payment kiosk through scrub that obscures the buildings before you. The grand entrance is revealed when you reach the kiosk. A wide stone path leads to an arch by a pond. The lovely buildings, in what I would call modern Tuscan monastic, are by Overland Partners and are designed to reflect regional architecture. They manage to be at once a little austere and welcoming, as befits an institution whose main purpose is education. Sandstone arches reflect Texas's Spanish heritage; limestone buildings, the classic German Hill Country style; and tin roofs and barns, the modern era.

Through the arch is the Central Complex, where you will find the gift shop and café and a hall dedicated to the memory of Mrs. Johnson. Beyond this rectangular courtyard are the Central Gardens that are the center's heart. Everything is labeled, and plants are set out in 23 themed gardens that demonstrate the enormous variety of flora in the state and provide inspiration for your own garden. Keep going, and you pass through the Pollinator Habitat Garden and onto the trail that leads to the Luci and Ian Family Garden, which was added in 2014 as a place where families can interact with nature. This path winds back to the Central Complex, and you can also explore two longer loops, the Woodland Trail and the Savanna Meadow Trail.

Cross the main area between the Central Complex and the Central Gardens to find the entrance to the longer trails. The John Barr Trail is a short loop that connects to the nearly mile-long Restoration Research Trail. If you have time for only one trail, choose the Mollie Steves Zachry Arboretum, where you will find examples of many common Texas trees. At last you will be able to distinguish a live oak from a cedar elm!

I can't recommend the wildflower center highly enough, whether you want a peaceful environment in which to chill quietly or are ready to really get to know the flowers, bushes, and trees of Texas. If you love it too, consider volunteering here, or support the center with an annual membership.

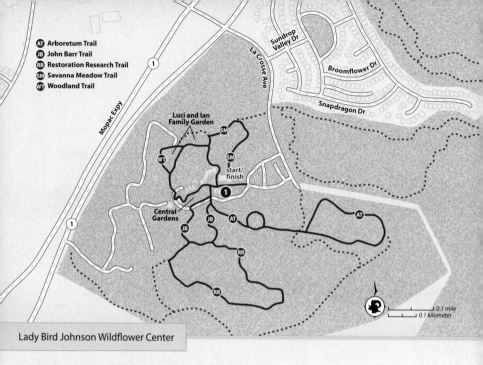

AT Arboretum Trail
JB John Barr Trail
RR Restoration Research Trail
SM Savanna Meadow Trail
WT Woodland Trail

Mopac Expy

La Crosse Ave

Sundrop Valley Dr

Broomflower Dr

Snapdragon Dr

Luci and Ian Family Garden

start/finish

Central Gardens

0.1 mile
0.1 kilometer

Lady Bird Johnson Wildflower Center

Point of Interest

1 Lady Bird Johnson Wildflower Center   4801 LaCrosse Ave., 512-232-0100, wildflower.org

20 Lady Bird Lake Boardwalks
New Views of the City

Above: *View of Austin's downtown from the boardwalk*

BOUNDARIES: S. First St., E. Riverside Dr., S. Pleasant Valley Road, Colorado River
DISTANCE: 4.8 miles
DIFFICULTY: Easy
PARKING: Paid parking at Long Center and Vic Mathias Shores (2-hour limit)
PUBLIC TRANSIT: Buses 10, 30, and 105 to stop 1567

Ann Butler met her husband, Roy, on a blind date while at the University of Texas (UT) in the 1940s. The ex–Navy man was studying law but left UT without a degree and started an automobile company that eventually became the biggest Lincoln dealership in Texas and Oklahoma. He then successfully bid to become the first Coors dealer in Central Texas. The Butlers became friends with President and Lady Bird Johnson when Roy sold LBJ a Lincoln, which Roy personally delivered to the Johnsons' ranch. He also owned the much-loved KASE and KVET radio stations that all of Austin listened to in the 1970s. In 1971 Roy ran for mayor, and during his time in office he spearheaded many of the changes that began to turn Austin from a sleepy college town into a major city, including the building of Mopac (see "Clarksville," page 51). He leased the building at Sixth and Lamar to Whole Foods and GSD&M, kick-starting the transformation of downtown. The same year he won election, the Butlers traveled to Europe for a mayors convention and met Lady Bird at the Savoy Hotel in London on the way home. The first lady, who had gotten involved in the Town Lake Beautification Project on her return to Austin from D.C., was very taken with the lovely trail along the River Thames. It was, the women agreed, so much prettier than the scruffy banks of the Colorado, whose south banks were just beginning to see serious development.

The Butlers began soliciting cash from rich friends in Houston and Dallas "because there was very little big money in Austin." Willie Nelson played a fundraising gala. Community gardening organizations were asked to assist, and in 2003 a nonprofit organization, The Trail Foundation, took over from the Town Lake Beautification Committee and began to work its small and large miracles along the trail. Usage exploded, and the problem of the 1-mile gap in the trail from South Congress Avenue to I-35 became more urgent. Property rights and steep cliffs meant that joggers were forced to divert along East Riverside Drive, a busy east–west cross street. Butch Smith, a city employee, had had a vision for the boardwalks more than 20 years ago, but it was 2007 before The Trail Foundation was able to get a bond package passed. Property owners provided easements, the foundation raised an additional $3 million, and the project was completed in two years, opening in 2014.

Ann Butler and Lady Bird Johnson simply wanted to make the city a prettier place, but what they built has become a defining piece of Austin. Renamed the Ann and Roy Butler Hike-and-Bike Trail in 2011, the trail is the de facto meeting point and destination for Austin's citizens, up to 15,000 of whom show up every day to jog, bike, hike, and play by the lakeshore. Mrs. Butler has every reason to be enormously proud of her shining achievement. *Note:* There is little shade on the boardwalks, so be prepared with a hat and sunscreen.

Walk Description

From your parking place, walk down to the west side of the South First Street Bridge past ❶ Vic Mathias Shores, formerly the east lawn of Auditorium Shores. This patch of grass is home to many of Austin's constant parade of festivals and concerts, including the long-running Aqua Festival (1962–1998), which Mathias helped found and whose Skipper Pin entry tokens were once an emblem of a real Austinite. In the 1970s Mathias was a member of the committee that worked on the plan for Lady Bird's trail. As CEO of the Chamber of Commerce, he worked to attract tech firms to the city to encourage UT students to stay in town after graduating. His legacy can be seen across Lady Bird Lake in the form of the ever-taller skyscrapers towering over the water. Not long ago the light-blue Frost Bank "owl" building was the king of downtown, but it was overtaken by the Austonian residential tower, which was soon to lose its status as tallest residential building west of the Mississippi to The Independent, immediately identifiable as the Jenga building, which itself is due to lose its crown to some impossibly tall structure.

Walk down to the Fannie Davis Town Lake Gazebo. This small structure, designed by John Nill, was the first result of the community's efforts to make a pleasant feature for the new body of water in its center: The Holly Street Power Plant, which was constructed in 1958, needed a cooling reservoir, and so the city built Longhorn Dam across the river in East Austin. The flood-prone Colorado became a wide lake, with a new, more stable and thus usable shoreline. In 1965, the National Association of Women in Construction presented plans for the gazebo, which was intended to honor their industry. It was eventually completed in 1970. Nill described his design as an "inverted morning glory." A large live oak has grown up next to the gazebo, which is set attractively between a pond and the lake on a small promontory, in an ideal spot from which to gaze on the works of those it was built to recognize.

The gazebo is a restful place, but it is at a busy spot on the trail. This popular access point has an exercise area and has become an unofficial doggy swimming hole. You can hear the constant crunch of gravel as runners and joggers plow by, plugged into their own universes.

The trail jumps onto the sidewalk as it goes under the South First Street bridge. Follow it through a hedge and onto the grounds of the Hyatt, where there is a dog-friendly Starbucks, and past the Capitol Cruises and Lone Star Riverboat piers. Head toward the Ann W. Richards Congress Avenue Bridge past a line of young cypresses, planted by The Trail Foundation to keep the bank stable. The most popular excursions on the cruise boats are the March–November evening bat-watching trips. Tourists gape as half a million Mexican free-tailed bats leave their roosts under the bridge to hunt for food, putting on a dazzling show of aerobatics as they go. The tangy odor of guano might make your eyes water as you walk below their bedroom.

The city opened a permanent bridge at Congress Avenue in 1887, but the flood-prone plains of the south shore remained undeveloped for many years. Moton H. Crockett, the Spinach King of Texas, used the area to grow crops in the early years of the 20th century, and during the 1950s sand was excavated from the riverbeds. With the construction of Longhorn Dam in 1960, buildings began to appear, and development still continues. New hotels and apartments are springing up in the area between Riverside and the lake, and the city has stepped up with a vision for the South Central Waterfront that includes a new park between Congress Avenue and East Bouldin Creek. This plan includes a bat-viewing pier, which would surely be popular, as currently people flock onto the bridge and spread themselves out over the lawn by the offices of the *Austin American-Statesman,* to your right as you continue. Here the gravel trail widens, and tall cypresses line the bank. By the time the trail comes to the end of the *Statesman'*s grounds it has become a tunnel of greenery. There are only flashes of water and the buildings across the lake and glimpses of the I-35 bridge ahead. Cyclists coast down a little incline just before the path narrows to pass close to some brown apartments.

Keep on, passing the wide lawn in front of the new Water Marq apartments, where you might see exercise classes and dogs playing (in case you forgot which city you are in). There's a convenient B-Cycle station here, at the boardwalk trailhead.

There are five overwater sections of boardwalk, two of which are quite short. The sections have galvanized steel supports and railings (which will not need painting) and concrete decking. They are roughly 10 feet wide and 6 feet above the water and are designed to have a minimal environmental impact. There are rest areas, observation points, and fishing piers. In general, traffic keeps to the right side of the path.

This first section is called Skyline Views and has indeed introduced Austin to new images of itself. Step onto the first observation platform for a better view of the city's ever-taller buildings outlined against the sky. Look back to the shore to notice where East Bouldin Creek flows into the lake from under a tree-covered channel. Sediment from the creek has created a sizable island. There is one more platform on this section, next to the promontory caused by Blunn Creek, whose main channel joins the lake by Joe's Crab Shack. The boardwalk continues across the wetlands at the bottom of a steep, wild chasm so covered in thick greenery as to be almost junglelike. Cantilevered walkways go up to an access point on East Riverside Drive.

The crunch of gravel underfoot tells you that you are back on land. Continue under steep cliffs through slivers of thick woods. The next short fragment of boardwalk, skirting a jutting wall of rock, is called the Woodland Trail. Return briefly to the banks, then head back out on the long section that leads past tall bluffs and under the three huge I-35 bridges. A metal bridge takes you over another ravine at Harper's Branch. More bridges lead up the small gorge to the busy junction of the highway and East Riverside Drive. Walk along a short section of gravel path to reach the longest stretch of overwater boardwalk, called the Waterfront Promenade. This part goes out quite a way into the lake, past more high cliffs. There are three larger piers here, partly shaded by curved metal panels, with a good view of Festival Beach on the other side of the lake.

These piers make good bird-watching stands. According to data from Cornell University and the National Audubon Society, whose database of bird sightings is at ebird.com, nearly 30 species were spotted in January and February 2018, including American coots, double-crested cormorants, northern cardinals, and Austin's iconic flock of monk parakeets that have survived since escaping from an RV park in the 1970s. The lake is known for its largemouth bass, and the third pier is marked as a fishing area.

This section ends, and the trail passes in front of the large AMLI South Shore apartment complex, at the junction of South Lakeshore Boulevard and East Riverside Drive. A connecting trail goes along the western side of the apartments to Riverside, where there is a food truck area. Palm trees along the shore enhance the holiday feel of this section, and if you have the urge to exercise in true Austin style, visit Live Love Paddle, a few steps farther along the bank, and rent a stand-up paddleboard. Once somewhat down-at-the-heels, the Lakeshore District, as it has come to be known, is now bustling with new apartments and restaurants. The city and The Trail Foundation are responding by improving facilities along this part of the trail as more people take advantage of it.

The last piece of boardwalk makes an elegant curve around an inlet and some pretty cream apartments to arrive at Lakeshore Park at the Boardwalk trailhead. An avenue of Mexican sycamores leads through a limestone-walled area, where there is more exercise equipment and another fishing pier. The small area is beautifully finished out. The Trail Foundation plans more improvements here, including a Rain Area, all designed to mitigate the environmental challenges of this fast-growing neighborhood.

Keep on for the last section of the walk. When I was here the air was full of white fluff from big cottonwood trees. To the right of the gravel path is a grove of trees planted in memory of lost loved ones. Keep left at a Y junction, passing between Epic SUP and the HI Austin Hostel. Enjoy the pollinator meadow planted to your left, cross a small inlet, and turn left, following the channel up a long, tree-covered peninsula that juts out into the widest part of the lake just before Longhorn Dam. The path jogs right at one pagoda and continues to the end of the peninsula through the thick muscadine vine–covered woods. The smell of the lake surrounds you even though the water is hidden until you reach another shelter at the end of the promontory. This park is ❷ Peace Point and is the end of our walk.

In front of you is Snake Island. To your right is the huge new Oracle building, and across the water is the site of the old Holly Plant. As we know, the lake was constructed as a cooling pond for that plant. Its four towers were once a landmark of East Austin. Local residents were more than relieved to see the polluting facility finally gone after a decommissioning and removal process that took 22 years. Though a few newer downtown buildings have now broached the horizon, the view from Peace Point to Snake Island cannot have changed much since 1960, when the dammed river first filled the new lake.

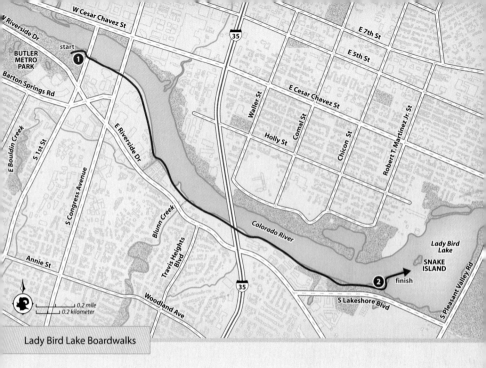

Lady Bird Lake Boardwalks

Points of Interest

1 Vic Mathias Shores at Town Lake Metropolitan Park 900 W. Riverside Dr.

2 Peace Point at Town Lake Metropolitan Park 2200 S. Lakeshore Blvd.

21 Mary Moore Searight Metropolitan Park
Exploring Slaughter Creek

Above: *Slaughter Creek, the southern boundary of the park*

BOUNDARIES: Slaughter Creek, W. Slaughter Lane, S. First St., David Moore Dr.
DISTANCE: 2.5 miles
DIFFICULTY: Easy
PARKING: At the park
PUBLIC TRANSIT: Buses 3 and 318 to stop 3766

❶ Mary Moore Searight Metropolitan Park spreads over the level ground between Slaughter Lane and Slaughter Creek, once farmland and now mostly covered with spare, low juniper woods. Our walk will take us around the southern portion, with a detour to a small dam on the creek. The northern part features an off-leash dog area (along South First Street); a popular disc golf course; and the Ralph DeClairmont RC Flying Field, home to the Hill Country Aeromodelers and off-limits to the general public. You might see and hear the model planes executing their

Backstory: Mary Moore Searight

Almost all the parks featured in this book owe their existence to individuals who were farsighted and generous enough to sell or donate their land for public use. And determined enough, as Mary Moore Searight must have been to have turned down several million-dollar offers for her land. Instead, the founding member of the Austin chapter of the Audubon Society sold 88 acres to the city and donated 206 more. Because the park comprises 344 acres, the city must have acquired more land from somewhere else, but Searight is the person we must thank, in particular for the access to Slaughter Creek. Searight's father, W. F. Moore, was appointed Texas's acting chief justice in 1939 and brought his family from Paris, Texas, to Austin to discharge his duties. Mary soon married Dan Searight, and they bought this land from the Slaughter family for cattle and hay. (Stephen F. Slaughter had come to the area from Kentucky in the 1830s and acquired the acreage from his neighbor Walter Wilson, which is how the Slaughter Fork of Onion Creek and Slaughter Lane got their names. Slaughter's neighbor to the north was William Cannon, immortalized in the eponymous thoroughfare, and Slaughter's son married Annie Eanes, from another famous Austin family.) Mary Moore Searight kept the ranch going for many years after her husband's death in the 1950s, but finally she moved back to Paris, where she died in 1996.

dives and loops over the treetops. The main walking trail makes a large loop around the southern section and incorporates a fitness trail of exercise apparatuses for an extra challenge. This is the Metro Trail. There is also an Equestrian Trail on which I have yet to see a horse. A tip of the hat to the Friends of Mary Moore Searight, the volunteer group that keeps the park in shape and the trails open. A stroll around this pleasant park and a few moments of rustic respite at the creek make a great pick-me-up at any time.

Walk Description

There are no trail maps at the park, but the main path is easy to follow, and Google Maps has most of the routes marked, so if you have your smartphone, you can use that application to guide you—a tip that works in many city parks. Face the playground and pavilion from the parking lot. Take the wide path in front of you to your right, your feet crunching on the gravel as you walk west along the edge of the trees. Follow this trail left to enter the woods and cross a branch of the creek, most likely a dry channel. Immediately go left at the next junction to keep on the main track, surfaced with asphalt. The right-hand path is the Equestrian Trail. Keep going as the wide path winds south through the juniper trees to meet the main loop. A juniper tree stands at the T junction. The more open area in front of you is full of wildflowers in the spring, and one can imagine Mary and Dan Searight baling hay in this field (see Backstory, page 117). At this junction you will see the first piece of the park's VitaCourse 2000 Fitness Trail, a step test where you can check your heart rate. Note the tree and the apparatus, as you will need to recognize them for the return.

It doesn't matter which way you go around the loop, but for the purposes of this walk, let's turn left to go clockwise. The path rambles in a large circle through juniper woods and meadows, occasionally passing the fitness apparatuses, where you can do your quota of pull-ups and knee raises. Just after the leg-lift station is a junction where you could go left onto the Equestrian Trail. This singletrack makes a wider wander south through the woods along the limestone bluffs above Slaughter Creek at the park's bottom tip, and if you keep left it will eventually bring you to the dam.

If you stay on the main loop you will eventually come to a multiway junction at the far end of a large field by a batting cage. The main asphalt track goes straight through this crossing. Turn left away from the field and keep straight on the obvious path toward a NO SWIMMING sign. Just past the sign go left down a rougher path that descends over exposed karst steps to the water's edge. Make your way east through the undergrowth a few yards to find the dam. One or two people may be casting their lines into the upstream pond from the concrete barrier. Relax here for a while to the sound of water flowing over the dam, and take in the views up and down the creek. The overgrown channel downstream is fun to explore, though there are no trails as such.

Climb back up the steps to the surfaced path; it continues west along the north bank of the creek, which at this point is as wide as a river. There are seats in the form of dice from which you can contemplate the creek and its wooded banks. Continue on a dirt trail to a bench, set at the sharp bend where the watercourse enters the park. From here you can complete the extra loop around the end of this wooded portion of the park or simply retrace your steps. Whichever way you go, you will come back to the same superjunction where you were before. Turn left onto the main loop, which curves through more woods and meadows around the edge of the park. Look for the lone juniper tree and the step-test apparatus that identify the left turn back to the parking lot.

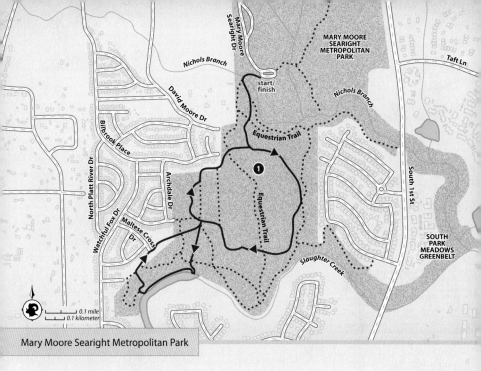

Mary Moore Searight Metropolitan Park

Point of Interest

❶ Mary Moore Searight Metropolitan Park 907 W. Slaughter Lane

22 Mayfield Park and Preserve
Palmettos and Swamps

Above: Taylor Slough flows into Lady Bird Lake.

BOUNDARIES: W. 35th St., Taylor Slough N., Pecos St.
DISTANCE: 0.7 mile
DIFFICULTY: Difficult, for some steep climbs
PARKING: At the preserve or on W. 35th St.
PUBLIC TRANSIT: None

The pristine white Mayfield-Gutsch house is the jewel of the 20-acre ❶ Mayfield Park and Preserve. The mansionette sits on a bluff above Lady Bird Lake, surrounded by a walled garden where you can wander among small lawns and a limestone patio with lily-covered fish ponds, enjoying the shade of oak trees and at least two species of palms. India blue and black-shouldered peacocks wander through the grounds. It's no surprise this is a popular spot for weddings and other gatherings. From the perimeter wall, there is a view down into the wilderness along

Backstory: The Mayfield Family

Born in Overton, Texas, Allison Mayfield was Texas secretary of state from 1894 to 1896 and served on the Railroad Commission for 26 years, from 1896 to 1922. He purchased this property in 1909 and used the small cottage that was there as a summer getaway. Mayfield's health was never good, and he died in 1923 after catching a cold on an official visit to Washington, D.C. The home and grounds passed to his only daughter, Mary, and she and her husband, Milton Gutsch, expanded the cottage and enlisted gardener Esteban Arredondo to help them create the botanical garden that surrounds the house. Ambitiously, Gutsch and Arredondo did all the masonry work themselves, but their inexperience led to some mistakes. In particular, they failed to put in foundations for the perimeter walls, and the Mayfield Foundation has recently had to rebuild them. Mary Mayfield Gutsch died in 1971, leaving the property to the city as a park. In 1994 it was added to the National Register of Historic Places.

Taylor Slough, and the manicured perfection of the house and terrace is a dramatic contrast to the jungle that surrounds it. Beyond the wall, thick woods hide steep steps and slippery cliffs and trails that explore the thriving greenery on the water's edge. Into this wilderness we shall venture!

Walk Description

From the parking lot, walk toward the house. Enter the enclosed area through an iron gate. Enjoy the peaceful shaded patio, which really is a paradise, given that the word comes from the ancient Persian for "walled garden." When you are ready, look for the entrance to the Bell Trail, which passes under a bell in the northeastern wall, directly opposite the gate through which you came in. This trail makes a steep descent into a different kind of paradise, the Garden of Eden that is the Taylor Slough valley. The plethora of palmettos are the damp forest's response to the palm trees surrounding the house. The woods are a thick tangle of Ashe juniper, cedar elm, and silk tassel, to name a few of the wealth of native flora. (There's a sign at the main trail entrance that will help you identify some of the different plants.) Volunteers are working hard at the endless and difficult task of ridding the preserve of common invasive species such as chinaberry, nandina (heavenly bamboo), and the all-pervasive ligustrum, or glossy privet. These species were imported from Asia as ornamental plants and have escaped into the wild, where they elbow out the Texas flora. For example, chinaberry leaves change the soil pH, making conditions unfavorable for native plants.

At the bottom of the hill is a marker post at a trail junction. It doesn't really matter which way you go, as you are unlikely to get lost in this small preserve. Either route has three water crossings.

The trails form a loop from the house to the parking lot, and are all connected. I like to take the left fork toward the East Creek Trail because it goes past craggy bluffs that are fun to scramble up. You will soon come to Taylor Slough, perhaps Austin's least-known creek, whose watershed is a triangle roughly bounded by Mopac (TX 1) and Balcones Drive, with its point just north of Ranch to Market Road 2222. The preserve's southern border is the inlet at the creek's confluence with Lake Austin. Ford Taylor Slough and keep left, climbing up over a ridge and down into a lost valley to cross a feeder branch that is bigger than the main channel. At a junction in a small clearing, look for steps to your left, which climb up to a ridge where Ashe juniper dominates. Follow the ridge to a point where you must scramble down to the end of the East Creek Trail. There's a swampy odor from the bayou. Go right, back to the junction, where you turn left. (You could leave out this ridgeline adventure and just turn right when you first come to this junction.)

Take the next left at a marker that says BELL TRAIL AND TAYLOR CREEK TRAIL, and make the third creek crossing. Climb up two sets of steps to a T junction, which is the entry point to the western section of the trails. The right fork goes back to the parking lot via the Meadow Loop and Main Trail. I recommend turning left onto the Creek Trail, which leads through a mix of juniper and cedar elm to meet the Lake Trail at the other end of the Meadow Loop. This path follows the banks of the inlet through the riot of flora (red oak, palmetto, and many more) by the water. Spur trails lead to the water's edge. The Lake View Trail, a loop off the Lake Trail, leads to a wooden platform with a view across the secluded inlet. When you get back to the Lake Trail, turn left and follow it back to the end of the parking lot. Ignore the path that heads to the Laguna Gloria Museum, as it ends at a locked gate in the fence around the museum grounds.

A palmetto on the bank of Taylor Slough

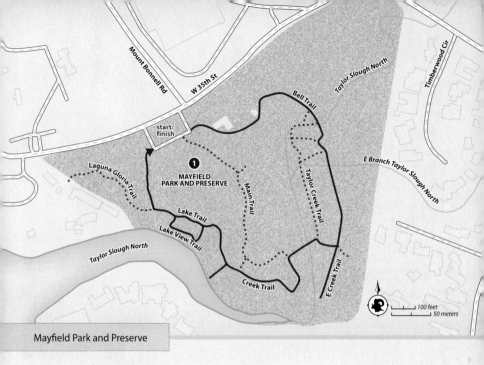

Mayfield Park and Preserve

Point of Interest

1 Mayfield Park and Preserve 3505 W. 35th St., 512-974-6700, mayfieldpark.org

23 Northern Walnut Creek Trail
Easy Scenic Views

Above: Walnut Creek in flood

BOUNDARIES: Walnut Creek from Lamar Blvd. to Metric Blvd.
DISTANCE: 2.9 miles
DIFFICULTY: Easy
PARKING: At Walnut Creek Metropolitan Park
PUBLIC TRANSIT: Bus 801 to stop 4548 (35-minute walk to the park)

If you are in North Austin, this is an easy escape to a picturesque chunk of the natural world. Walnut Creek Metropolitan Park sprawls across nearly 300 acres to the north and south of a pretty section of this long creek that roughly maps out Austin's east and north boundaries. Wells Branch flows down through the eastern side and joins Walnut Creek in the park. There are well-used softball fields and a basketball court, along with the normal quota of picnic tables and children's playgrounds. The main draw of the park itself has up to now been the tangled knots of dirt trails (one section is actually called the Tangle of Trails) south of the main creek and east of Wells Branch. Some steep and rocky, these trails are popular with nature lovers, mountain bikers, BMX riders, and, most of all, dog lovers because the trails do not require dogs to be leashed and feature plenty of creek access. But you don't have to bring your bike and water shoes to have a good time here, as since 2016 the main parking lot is now the beginning of the smooth new North Walnut Creek Hike and Bike Trail, a companion to the Southern Walnut Creek Trail (see page 149). Fingers crossed, these two trails will eventually be joined into a huge hiking-and-biking superhighway. Both trails have become popular quickly, for obvious reasons. They are easy to follow; are great for walking, running, and bicycling; and provide access to some of the best of Austin's natural beauty. This northern trail begins in the cedar forests and creekside woods of Walnut Creek Metropolitan Park and journeys across steep canyons with views of the rocky watercourse and surrounding country. The trailhead is at the western end of the main parking lot, and from there this Cadillac of a trail goes just over 3 miles to the eastern end of Balcones District Park. For this out-and-back walk we suggest a turnaround point at Gracywoods Neighborhood Park, but you can extend the route to take in the pretty creekside section just past Metric Boulevard. Although the route is almost always bordered by dense greenery, the path itself lacks any shade, so come prepared with a hat and sunscreen.

Walk Description

There's not much in the way of directions necessary for this walk, as all you have to do is follow the wide concrete path as it winds northwest toward Mopac. The first section begins with an impressive ramp, leading into the juniper woods of ❶ Walnut Creek Metropolitan Park. Here the trail is crisscrossed by several dirt paths that disappear into the dense cedar thickets. Come to the first of many bridges, all of the same design (they are made in Minneapolis), which crosses the overgrown Tar Branch. The second bridge is a long, high span over Walnut Creek itself, here as wide as a river. Pause for the view and a picture of the deep, tree-covered valley.

From this point on, dogs must be leashed. You will see dog walkers, runners, bicyclists, and families with strollers. The trail winds to the right, goes under some transmission lines, and then begins to climb to a higher ridge. The creek is in a deep, forested gorge to your right. Soon you will see apartment buildings ahead to the left, and then a long bridge suspended high over the bushes. For the mildly adventurous or curious there's a very short side trip down a track to the right just before the crossing; this brings you to the top of the steep drop for a dizzying view down into the valley. The bridge looks like it should be going over a brook high in some

Other Trails in Walnut Creek Metropolitan Park

To describe a route through Walnut Creek Metropolitan Park's dirt trails would require a complex and confusing list of directions, so my suggestion is to strike out and explore this rough terrain for yourself. To get to the southern section you need to ford the creek, so be prepared to get your feet wet, and be aware that the water can be high and fast after heavy rainfall. It's a grand opportunity to get lost for an hour or so, and all the better with a dog as your companion. Access to this section is at the back of the first parking lot (to the left) off Walnut Creek Park Road.

mountains. Look down to your right to catch a glimpse of Walnut Creek, glistening at the bottom of its gorge. Take a photo of the view over the treetops, the most scenic vista on this walk.

The trail rounds a corner and emerges into ❷ Gracywoods Neighborhood Park, an expanse of lawn nestled into the curve of the creek and dotted with shade trees. A gazebo offers a vantage point to look down at the rocky stream. This park is almost 2 miles from the parking lot at Walnut Creek Metropolitan Park and is a respectable turnaround spot. It has trail access and parking. If you continue at least another 0.5 mile past Metric Boulevard, you will find a section where the trail is right by the creek, and the walk is through delightful bottomland woods of hackberry and cedar elm. There are three more bridges. After the first there is a wide curve through a pleasant field by an apartment complex, but the next two crossings come in quick succession and provide pleasant vantage points to study the trees and the water until you are ready to head back and face the world.

View of Walnut Creek from Walnut Creek Trail

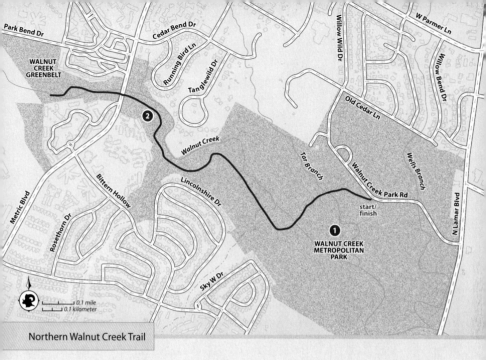

Northern Walnut Creek Trail

Points of Interest

1 Walnut Creek Metropolitan Park   12138 N. Lamar Blvd.
2 Gracywoods Neighborhood Park   12133 Metric Blvd.

24 Onion Creek Loop at McKinney Falls
Woods and Waterfalls in Austin's Backyard

BOUNDARIES: Onion Creek, McKinney Falls Pkwy., E. William Cannon Dr.
DISTANCE: 2.8 miles
DIFFICULTY: Easy
PARKING: At the park (follow signs to Upper Falls)
PUBLIC TRANSIT: None

The Texas Parks and Wildlife Department touts ❶ McKinney Falls State Park as "practically Austin's backyard," and the catchphrase rings true. Southeast Austin is slowly beginning to surround the park, whose famous waterfalls are a favorite escape of residents. McKinney Falls is the most easterly of the string of in-city recreational areas along Onion Creek and still the largest, though the new Onion Creek Metropolitan Park will be almost as big once it is fully open. There are two falls in the park, Upper and Lower, and at both places the stream tumbles over wide dimpled-limestone ledges into pools that are well-known swimming and fishing spots. The creek has no major dams, and these falls can be raging torrents or sad trickles and can change swiftly. The park has two hike-and-bike trail systems. The more challenging trail begins on the other side of the Lower Falls, and the farthest loop leads to bluffs along a wild stretch of Williamson Creek, which flows into the park and joins Onion Creek at the Lower Falls. That's a wonderful but lengthy route, but for our route we will stroll around the 2.8-mile Onion Creek Hike and Bike Trail, an easy asphalt-surfaced loop trail that follows the creek's course through the rich wooded bottomland and then climbs to the rolling juniper savanna for the return journey. You will pass some historical structures: the remains of a cabin and some stone walls from the 19th century.

Walk Description

Start by the Upper Falls and the Smith Visitor Center, which is closed. Go down a short incline, toward the creek, which here tumbles or dribbles over the waterfall. Go left into the picnic area, where the inviting tables claim patches of shade under the tall trees. Ramble through the picnic and primitive camping areas. The woods thicken as the path wanders closer to the creek, a glimpse of brown through the dense greenery. Keep an eye out for the painted bunting, a small, colorful songbird that nests in the park through the summer. The trail passes a stone embankment on the left, built to prevent further erosion of the hillside. A small foot trail also leads down to the creek on the right, and here the main path climbs sharply away from the water. When you reach the plateau, a park bench offers a place to sit and rest. Cardinals dart and wolf-whistle around you, and you might see a roadrunner dashing across the trail. The surroundings are the familiar Hill Country mix of oak and cedar, which each predominate in turn.

The trail makes a loop to cross a small feeder branch then passes along the park's southern edge. This used to border a field, and you would never have known that you were at the park boundary, but now a new neighborhood has sprung up across the fenceline. For the lucky people living there, the park really is their backyard. Keep walking and you'll see a stone wall that was the property boundary, dating from the mid-1800s. At a fork, another bench allows for a rest and a chance to observe nature. In the spring, mama deer give birth in the grassy areas, and you might spy the fawns hiding under the bushes or hear them calling to their mothers. These babies are not lost and should be left alone.

More rock wall appears just after a little creek crossing, and this section still serves as the park boundary, though it was originally built for horse corrals. Thomas McKinney, who owned this ranch, had a keen interest in horses, apparently inherited from his grandfather, and he raised and

Backstory: Thomas McKinney

State senator, rancher, horse breeder, trader, and privateer: Thomas McKinney was all of these, securing himself a lasting place in Texas history. Originally from Kentucky, he and a partner helped finance the Texas Revolution, and McKinney used his own schooner to capture a Mexican boat. He was a cofounder of the city of Galveston, but once the revolution was over he acquired 40,000 acres at the confluence of Onion and Williamson Creeks. This land had been sold to McKinney's business partner Michael Menard by Mexican land speculator and government official Santiago del Valle, and Menard in turn sold it to McKinney. In 1843 McKinney divorced his first wife, Nancy, and married the 21-year-old Anna Gibbs, and in a couple of years the couple moved from Galveston to Travis County, looking to settle down after the turbulent years of revolution. But the Civil War brought financial ruin, and McKinney's health began to fail. He died in his home in 1873, and Anna sold the property to James Smith, whose grandson donated the portion that is now the park to the state. Long before Thomas McKinney, El Camino Real de los Tejas passed through the park on its way from the Rio Grande to Louisiana, and you can still see wagon tracks preserved in the limestone at the Lower Falls.

raced them. The ranch had extensive exercise and training areas. He even traveled to Mexico in his own steamboat to trade horses. At the point where the trail crosses the park road, you can see to your right the ruins of the small house that was the two-room home of McKinney's horse trainer. His name was John Van Hagen, and he lived here for more than 20 years until McKinney died, when he moved to New York (for more on McKinney, see Backstory, above).

The last section of the hike goes through taller hardwoods, which you exit at the parking lot next to the Smith Visitor Center, where we began. For extra credit, take the Rock Shelter Interpretive Trail to see Old Baldy, a 500-year-old cypress tree, and the eponymous overhang—listed on the National Register of Historic Places—where people have sheltered for more than 4,000 years. This primitive trail starts close to the small parking lot behind the Smith Visitor Center and follows the edge of the cliffs above Onion Creek. Look for the wooden walkway that leads to Old Baldy, a tall, very old cypress that towers over a small feeder canyon. The shelter is a little farther on. You can continue to reach the enormous limestone outcrop by the Lower Falls and even cross those falls to follow the Homestead Trail 100 yards or so to the remains of McKinney's home.

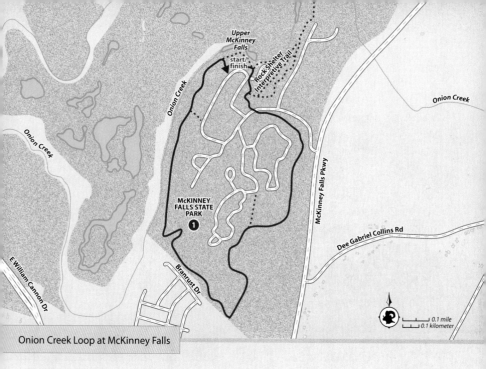

Onion Creek Loop at McKinney Falls

Point of Interest

❶ McKinney Falls State Park 5808 McKinney Falls Pkwy., 512-243-1643,
tpwd.texas.gov/state-parks/mckinney-falls

25 Red Bud Isle Trail
The Isle of Dogs

Above: The view from the end of Red Bud Isle

BOUNDARIES: Lady Bird Lake, Redbud Trail
DISTANCE: 0.6 mile
DIFFICULTY: Easy
PARKING: There is a small parking lot at the park that fills up quickly. If it is full, try parking on Lake Austin Blvd. and walk down Redbud Trail to the entrance.
PUBLIC TRANSIT: Bus 663 to stop 4985

❶ Red Bud Isle is one of the few places in the city where dogs can run, play, and swim off-leash, and if you are an Austinite with a dog who has not yet experienced the joys of this leafy islet, then you need to put Dante in the Subaru pronto and head on down here. It is certainly paradise for canines, but to call these 18 acres a dog park would not do Red Bud Isle justice. The long, narrow island practically fills the river below the Tom Miller Dam, and in fact is made of debris from that structure's predecessor (for more on the failed former dam, see Backstory, page 134). The imposing cliffs of Rollingwood tower over the western bank, and the view downriver from the end of the island is an Austin classic. In the spring the island's woods are dotted with the pink blossoms of *Cercis canadensis* var. *texensis,* the Texas redbud, a native bush that is a source of shelter and sustenance for bees, butterflies, and birds. You certainly should not come here if you do not like dogs, but for the rest of us it's a chance to enjoy both a dive into nature and the delighted reactions of the pups running, jumping, and barking happily.

Walk Description

Even the walk is kind of dog-shaped, minus the legs, consisting of a loop from the head, which is the parking lot, to the long tail that leads to the park's sharp point. At the peninsula's heart is an elevated open area, perfect for romping. The island's belly pooches out a bit toward the eastern bank of the Colorado, and I guess the route is a dachshund, as there are some very short legs leading down to the water. The trails are flat, wide, and attractively surfaced with pink gravel. The Friends of Red Bud Isle have added many improvements, including erosion control, a split-rail fence, and an information board, and in general this park, despite the heavy dog use, is always clean and well tended.

The shady paths wander under a tunnel of varied greenery that includes cedar elm, oak, and a few juniper trees. Cypress trees and the occasional sycamore line the banks at the edge of the dense thickets. Although human swimming is prohibited, volunteers have fashioned some doggy access points, and these also provide views for people of the lake's wooded banks on either side of the island. To the west, those towering layers of rock rise up to the cliff's-edge mansions of the Stratford Hills neighborhood, and the wild and inaccessible walls continue around the downstream bend. This vista is one of the most dramatic examples of the city's contiguity with nature. The trees lining the northern shore of the lake hide some University of Texas apartments from view. A tangled knot of thick cypress roots slithering under the surface marks the end of the island, and sitting here, despite the clifftop houses, you could easily imagine yourself in a place far distant from the city. Downtown is out of sight around the river bend, and only the slight thrum of traffic is a reminder that you are in the city. A 30-minute walk to the end of this enchanted isle makes for an uplifting start to anyone's day.

As mentioned, the small parking lot fills up quickly, and you might consider arriving via alternative transport, such as a kayak or stand-up paddleboard, both of which you can rent from the Rowing Dock (rowingdock.com) on Stratford Drive. The paddle up the river to Red Bud Isle and back from there takes a couple of hours, and it's a great thing to do in the morning before it gets too hot. And you can certainly bring your dog!

Backstory: The Austin Dam Debacle

Red Bud Isle is a remnant of one of Austin's greatest failures, the Austin Dam, which the city went into great debt to build in the early 1890s. Smaller pieces of the old dam, built across the river where the Tom Miller Dam is now, can still be seen in the river. The dam (which William Porter, also known as O. Henry, wrote about in his *Rolling Stone* paper; see "Austin's Mexico," page 4) was designed to catapult Austin to success as a center for cotton milling. The lake that was created was dubbed Lake McDonald after the mayor at the time, a great booster of the project. San Antonio businessman George Brackenridge bought land below it, hoping to make money selling mill sites, but the project was badly thought out. It turned out that the river flow was too uneven for mills, at times barely sufficing to power the city's electric streetcars and the famous Moonlight Towers. The structure itself was poorly built, and McDonald meddled in the process so much that the original engineer quit in frustration. In addition, the spot chosen was exactly where the Balcones Fault goes under the river. It was not much of a surprise when the dam gave way in the huge storms of April 7, 1900, with a sound "like a gunshot." Eight workers drowned, and McDonald's lake was no more. The city tried to rebuild, but a later flood did yet more damage, and the ruins remained a sore reminder of the debacle until the Lower Colorado River Authority (LCRA) built Tom Miller Dam in 1940. Not everything turned out badly, though. Brackenridge donated his land to the University of Texas, which still uses it for student housing, and the city, having gotten accustomed to electrical power, formed Austin Energy to better manage its power needs.

Stick envy at Red Bud Isle

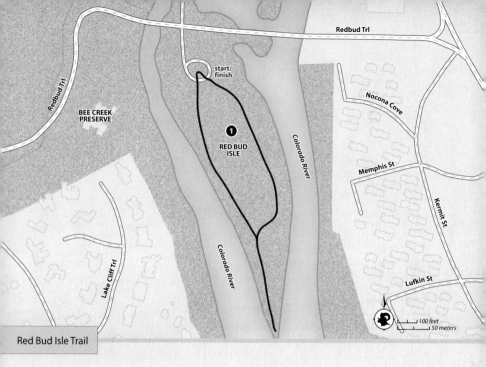

Point of Interest

1 Red Bud Isle 3401 Redbud Trail, 512-974-6700, austintexas.gov/department/parks-and-recreation

26 Shoal Creek Greenbelt
The Comanche Trail

Above: An oak tree grows at Custer's Field in Pease District Park.

BOUNDARIES: W. Cesar Chavez St./W. Sixth St., W. 24th St., Shoal Creek
DISTANCE: 4.1 miles
DIFFICULTY: Easy
PARKING: Street parking downtown; AMLI garage at Second and Nueces; or on Parkway at Custer's Field
PUBLIC TRANSIT: Buses 4 and 5 to stop 1970

Shoal Creek formed the western boundary of Judge Edwin Waller's original city plan in 1839, although the meandering watercourse did not conform to the straight lines of Waller's grid, taking a small bite out of the southwest corner of the rectangle. Back then the land beyond the creek's western banks was Comanche territory, and the track up the creek was known as the Comanche Trail. The Indians must have looked down incredulously from what is now Castle Hill as the new city was built. These days the watershed, which stretches from Braker Lane to the river, is a very urban

13 square miles, home to tens of thousands of families, and today's challenge is to allow the creek and its banks to flourish in the face of the city's nonstop growth. The Shoal Creek Conservancy, a nonprofit group that presents itself as the steward of the creek, has a vision to realize that goal through a network of parks along its length. In July 2018 they released a draft of the Shoal Creek Trail Action Plan, proposing major extensions and improvements to the current 3.9-mile trail to connect it to North Walnut Creek Trail. As the draft says, a healthy habitat with hike-and-bike trails and green spaces will improve life for all Austin residents, whether plant, animal, or human. This easy out-and-back walk will explore the 2 miles of the trail to the northern end of Pease Park.

Walk Description

The whole trail is 3.9 miles long, from Lady Bird Lake to 38th Street, but there is currently a detour from 24th Street to Gaston Avenue due to the last phase of the Shoal Creek Restoration project. The city is working on streambank stabilization, adding hike-and-bike trails, and general landscape restoration. Start by the new main Austin Public Library at 710 W. Cesar Chavez St., and walk up the trail on the western bank. Take in the spectacular views of downtown, where skyscrapers compete to touch the sky. Just before you get to the Sixth Street Bridge, take the ramp to the street. On the north side of the street is a historical marker commemorating the Wood Street Settlement on Shoal Creek. As people moved to the new capital, they needed servants and handymen, and freed African Americans came to Austin to find work. They settled just outside the city along the creek's western bank. After the infamous 1928 city plan moved African Americans to East Austin, Mexican American families settled here (see "Austin's Mexico," page 4), and the community persisted until the 1970s, holding out against both flooding and prejudice. According to the sign, the last houses from the community were demolished as recently as 2014.

Return to the trail via the access path by which you came up to the street. Turn left when you get to the trail proper, passing under the historic ❶ Sixth Street Bridge. Built in 1887, it is older than the State Capitol and is one of the oldest bridges in the state. It was built as wide as the street to accommodate wagons and mule-drawn streetcars. The three-arched masonry structure replaced an older iron bridge and was key to the city's first big expansion west along the river and into Clarksville, which was at that time a community of freed African Americans living in the rough high ground west of the city. (See "Clarksville," page 51). Judge Waller insisted on naming the cross streets after trees, rather than numbering them, and Pecan Street, as Sixth was then called, was the city's major east–west thoroughfare and commercial center. As the city grew and development began to the west, a better bridge over Shoal Creek became an urgent priority. In particular, James Raymond, a financier who owned a lot of land west of the creek and was anxious to develop it, lobbied for its construction. On March 21, 1887, the council passed an ordinance allotting $6,126.20 "for the erection of a double-arched stone bridge over Shoal Creek on West Pecan Street." The same ordinance called for the removal of the old iron bridge and the construction of a corresponding bridge over Waller Creek at East Avenue. The bridge has three arches, as mentioned, so somewhere along the way the plans got changed. The bridge survived the 1981 Memorial Day flood and looks good to hold up for another 100 years or more.

Past the bridge, the creek has been somewhat channelized, and the new Austin towers over its eastern banks, but by Ninth Street it has regained its natural character. The concrete trail crosses the creek as it goes under the bridge and then passes through ❷ Duncan Neighborhood Park, a sloping field with a few benches. Through the greenery you might see people enjoying the Shoal Creek Saloon's patio on the opposite bank. Keep north and pass under the 10th and 12th Street bridges, then take a moment to look north across 15th Street, the city's original northern boundary. The ridgeline that marks the edge of Judges Hill and West Campus is the eastern side of this steep-sided valley that disappears north into what was at one time dangerous territory. Nowadays there is a chance to experience a different kind of danger at the Heath Eiland and Morgan Moss BMX Skate Park, built on the site of a recreation center that was damaged in the 1981 flood. Eiland died in a skateboarding accident as a teenager, while Moss, a talented photographer active in the skateboarding community, was killed in a car wreck at the age of 25. Just north of the skate park is House Park Stadium, a much-loved facility built in 1939 on land donated by Edward M. House, a diplomat who served under Woodrow Wilson, and used by Austin Independent School District.

The concrete path continues north along Shoal Creek Boulevard, going under the low Lamar Boulevard bridge and next to the high 15th Street roadway, which spans the entire valley. For a brief stretch you are on the Lamar Boulevard sidewalk, but look for the left turn into ❸ Pease District Park, crossing the creek on an arched iron-trestle bridge. Look right for a view north along the watercourse exploding with greenery. The park was established in 1875 on land bought by Texas governor Elisha Pease. It and the Shoal Creek Greenbelt comprise 84 acres, and the remainder of this walk is through this park. Lack of funding, flooding, and intense foot traffic had an increasingly detrimental effect on the land until 2008, when concerned neighbors and friends of the park formed the Pease Park Conservancy, a nonprofit group that organized volunteer days and worked with the city to save the amenity. Wander around the popular southern end, known as Kingsbury Commons, where there are picnic

Backstory: Greenbelt Benefactors

Let's remember and thank Governor Elisha Pease, the man who donated a portion of his 365-acre Woodlawn Plantation property to the city to be used as parkland, and Janet Fish, an Austin native of boundless energy and enthusiasm whose father was Walter E. Long, Austin's Father of City Planning. In the 1950s Fish took it upon herself (and drafted her family into her plan) to rebuild a section of the Comanche Trail that had disappeared in the 1930s. "She was driving an old Plymouth station wagon, and my father had given her money to go buy a new car," recalls her son Andy. Instead, Fish hired a bulldozer and spent the next four years grading a new trail from the north end of Pease Park to Gaston Avenue. Apparently the weeds were so high that she threw her hat in the air so that the bulldozer could follow her. Anyone who walks along the Shoal Creek greenbelt owes both of these people a moment of gratitude.

tables and a Tudor-style cottage from the 1930s, as well as volleyball courts and a new splash pad for kids. The park's iconic gates stand on the south side of Kingsbury Street, the park's southern boundary. The gravel trail goes north on the creek side of Big Field, a large open space that is home to one of Austin's most iconic activities: the annual Eeyore's Birthday festival of face-painting, acrobatics, and drum circles. A forest of Ashe juniper, hackberry, and cedar elm covers the slope west of the field. At the end of Big Field, the path climbs into this forest and then descends in Custer's Field. Stop at the bottom and take in the southern vista of limestone bluffs along the creek. The Pease Park Conservancy and the City of Austin have done a great deal of work to restore the natural beauty of the park and creek. Custer's Field is so named because General Custer bivouacked his troops here during the winter of 1865–1866. Sadly, many of the men perished from cholera; their bodies were uncovered by later flooding. A large live oak, Custer's Oak, is the arboreal centerpiece of this area. Reportedly, Robert E. Lee also camped by the creek with his men during the Civil War. Custer's Field ends at 24th Street, about 2 miles from the starting point, and this is the turnaround for today's walk.

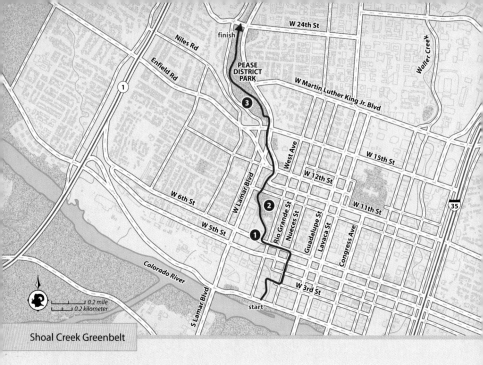

Shoal Creek Greenbelt

Points of Interest

1. Sixth Street Bridge Sixth St. and Shoal Creek, 512-474-2412, shoalcreekconservancy.org
2. Duncan Neighborhood Park Ninth St. and West Ave., 512-974-6700, austintexas.gov/department/parks-and-recreation
3. Pease District Park 1100 Kingsbury St., 512-777-1632, peasepark.org

27 South Congress Avenue
SoCo Shopping and Dining

Above: Stop at Güero's on South Congress Avenue for iconic Mexican food.

BOUNDARIES: S. Congress Ave. from Nellie St. to Johanna St.
DISTANCE: 0.6 mile
DIFFICULTY: Easy
PARKING: Back-in parking along South Congress, or the parking garage behind Perla's. Parking in the surrounding neighborhoods is severely restricted.
PUBLIC TRANSIT: Bus 1 to stop 576

When James Milton Swisher subdivided the family farm along the San Antonio road in what was not yet South Austin, he reserved 120 feet for the new neighborhood's central avenue. This generous choice gave the street a noble air that emphasizes and responds to the view down the hill to the Capitol. But in the late 1800s crossing the river was difficult over an inadequate bridge, and South Austin community leaders began agitating for better access. On April 3, 1910, crowds of people came to walk across the newly opened concrete structure that you see today, a improvement that contributed greatly to the success of General William Harwood Stacy's new Travis Heights addition. The area grew rapidly, and with the rise of automobile tourism, motels, gas stations, and restaurants began to appear alongside the barber shops and grocery stores that catered to the local clientele. Even when I-35 was built, people turned off the highway to experience the view from the wide boulevard, and by 1952 there were 21 motels between Ben White Boulevard and the river. The Twin Oaks shopping center at Oltorf opened in 1954, its set-back design and large parking lot denoting it as one of the first malls to rely on automobile traffic. Other businesses included the Nighthawk Diner at Barton Springs Road, where in 1958 Harry Akin became the first white business owner to serve an African American. Akin became mayor 10 years later, and under his guidance the city finally passed laws forbidding segregation.

The interstate highway did eventually take its toll on through traffic, and in the 1960s and '70s the area started to decline. With so many motels, the street became known for prostitution and vice, a reputation that survived well into '90s. But the Armadillo opened in 1970 at Barton Springs and Riverside Avenue, becoming a mecca for longhairs, hippies, and like-minded folks. These people began to move into the South River City and Bouldin neighborhoods and established the relaxed, bohemian atmosphere that these neighborhoods still retain. Small businesses opened along the avenue, taking advantage of cheap rent, and the SoCo of today began to gel. The area's success means the rent has gone up, but many of South Congress's signature homegrown enterprises have held on and mostly flourished as the street has become a major tourist attraction. There are so many fascinating places to explore and investigate along this street, and I have cherry-picked the most iconic and interesting businesses it has to offer. Bear in mind that stores come and sometimes go—I've (mostly) chosen established places, but things do change. Given the wealth of options available, this walk sticks to the west sidewalk, but in passing I'll point out some places on the other side of the street that you can check out if you wish, perhaps on the way back down.

Walk Description

Start at the southwest corner of Nellie and South Congress, the north end of the long line of historic commercial buildings that goes to Annie Street. Our first stop is Patti and Jerry Ryan's ❶ Heritage Boot Co. They sell handmade custom boots from a third-generation bootmaker in León, Mexico, a city that has long been a center of the leather industry. The retro designs are bold, stylish, and available only online or in the store, where a Boot Maven will guide you to the right decision. Even if you do not have $1,000 or more to spend on footwear, step inside to experience the sight (and smell) of so many beautiful cowboy boots in one place. I was very tempted by the Blanco County version in cream American bison.

Next door is the edgy ❷ **Blackmail Boutique**. Here you will find noirish clothes, jewelry, and T-shirts with cynical epithets. There is more stuff for girls than guys, so if you are (or know) a Goth-leaning female, you'll likely find a top or dress that adds perfectly to your (or their) look.

A few steps south is the landmark ❸ **Austin Motel**, with its notoriously priapic sign (from 1938) that boldly states the hotel's indelible motto, SO CLOSE YET SO FAR OUT, a phrase that has established itself in the Austin vernacular. The motel has an ancient connection with Blackmail, as the land on which it was built belonged to German immigrants Leonard and Frances Eck. The couple opened the first store south of the river in the building the boutique now occupies. Eck's daughter Jennie Eck Stewart expanded her father's business, and she and her husband, Earnest, opened the motel as a response to the increased tourist traffic along the avenue. It has never closed and usually sells out on weekends and during events. It is now owned by Austin hotelier Liz Lambert's Bunkhouse Group, who have recently refurbished the rooms in bright retro styles. Other amenities include a kidney-shaped pool and lido deck. Joann's Fine Foods, the restaurant attached to the hotel, is a new venture from restaurateur Larry McGuire that serves California Tex-Mex–style food. It replaced longtime favorite Snack Bar, which closed in 2016, the owners declaring that they found the Austin dining scene too tumultuous.

Lambert's group also owns the next two stops, just across James Street. Stop and take the quintessential Austin selfie at the "I love you so much" mural on the side of ❹ **Jo's Coffee**, art that has taken on a life of its own in a million photos and memes. The original mural was by Lambert's partner at the time, singer-songwriter Amy Cook, who painted it overnight as a declaration of her feelings. It's been redone and trademarked, and everybody's moved on, but the message still resonates. There's often a wait to take photos and a line around the corner to order coffee drinks and the excellent sandwiches, but in the mornings Jo's is still the place where locals get their Iced Turbos (Jo's signature sweet, creamy, cold coffee drink) and sweet rolls and conversation. The Sinner's Brunch on Sunday mornings is a good time to relax to down-home sounds as you watch the world go by from behind a beer.

Jo's is in the parking lot of the ❺ **Hotel San José**, a sleek boutique inn whose stylish crannies are seductively obscured behind tall hedges, though the cool green walls and red tiles are a giveaway to the classy interior. In the '90s Lambert, an Odessa native, was a lawyer at the Texas attorney general's office looking for a change. She took the plunge, and her 1996 purchase and renovation of the worse-than-seedy San José was a big sign that something might be made to happen on the shabby avenue. She hired San Antonio architects Lake/Flato and, together with friends R. L. Fletcher and Jamey Garza, obsessed over "almost every piece of furniture, every paint color, and every hook," she said. "Literally, we worked through the design of the black steel bathroom hooks together." A stay in one of the minimalist rooms might not be on your agenda, but you can slide on into the hotel courtyard for a snack and a michelada, chilling in the chic surroundings to mellow tunes from local DJs. Before she bought the place, Lambert and her friend Steve Wertheimer would gaze at the motel and imagine the possibilities from outside Wertheimer's Continental Club across the street. The Continental Club has its own long story, which you can read about in "Austin's Music Landmarks, Part 1" (page 21), but if you are not going to return to SoCo, you should cross the street and take a peek at that legendary Austin institution.

South of Gibson Street is a modern complex where you can find our next three destinations, the first being the oak-shaded patio of ❻ **Perla's** seafood restaurant and oyster bar, a perfect spot for a cool lunch on a hot summer's day. Enjoy a selection of oysters on the half shell from the cold bar, together with an oyster shooter and seasoned saltine crackers. In its 10 years or so of existence, Perla's has rightly cemented its place on the list of Austin's most recommended restaurants. Naturally there's a connection with the Hotel San José. Larry McGuire, CEO of the company that owns Perla's (and Joann's Fine Foods), got his break working with Liz Lambert's brother Lou. Together McGuire and Lambert opened Lambert's Downtown Barbecue, and McGuire was launched on his mission to put Austin on the map as a food town. Since then he and partner Tom Moorman have opened a steady stream of excellent restaurants, three of them on South Congress. The third is June's All Day, a casual café and bistro at Annie Street that made *Food & Wine*'s 2017 Best New Restaurants list.

Walk down the breezeway next to Perla's to ❼ **Service Menswear**, where, as the name suggests, you will find sensible clothes for guys from brands like Levi's, RVCA, and Ray-Ban. They carry Florsheim boots and shirts from Naked and Famous, so you (or your guy) can be kitted out in proper masculine gear in no time, especially since the friendly staff make a point of offering excellent, well, service.

There's usually a queue out the door to order at ❽ **Hopdoddy Burger Bar,** the Austin-based chain that is expanding across the south and west and that epitomizes the casually military style of chain dining that has become so common. Stand in line, get a beer (or margarita) on the way to the back to order your burger, take your number, sit down, and wait. The food comes quickly and the burgers are excellent, both the bun and meat tasty and fresh, made from scratch on-site. They come in a variety of tantalizing styles, including the Au Jus and my favorite, the Llano Poblano, a spicy take on a bacon cheeseburger. You can try versions with bison, tuna, or chicken, or sample the Impossible, Hopdoddy's vegetarian patty. That name is a play on the booze and burgers concept: hops = beer, and *doddy* is apparently Scots slang for cow.

Our next stop (and next door) is one of Austin's holy of holies. Rob and Cathy Lippincott's **9** Güero's Taco Bar is so settled into South Congress that it's hard to remember that until 1993 it was on Oltorf Street, where Curra's is now. Some of you will remember this spot as the Central Feed and Seed Co., and that name is still on the building. The Lippincotts opened their taqueria in 1986 and guided the business through the move and into the hands of daughters Lyle and Bette, who now run the iconic restaurant, which serves margaritas, tacos, and number one dinners to an endless line of happy customers. Enjoy music in the restaurant and in the shady Oak Garden that you will have passed on the short walk from Hopdoddy. Just like a selfie at Jo's, eating at Güero's is an essential Austin experience. What's a *güero*? A gringo, *por supuesto*!

What's that delicious aroma? Pause to salivate in the direction of food writer–turned–Queen of Pies Jen Scoville Strickland's Home Slice Pizza across the way, whose New York–style slices are so authentically delicious that you might want to risk crossing the street to try one.

Cross Elizabeth Street for our next three stops, all in the next block north and none of them restaurants. **10** Lucy in Disguise with Diamonds has been the ultimate dress-up store since 1984, when it opened as two smaller stores, Lucy in Disguise and Electric Ladyland. You can get pretty much any costume or accessory you can imagine in this 8,000-square-foot box of wonders, from a phony cast to a Joker mask. Transform yourself or your kid into an elephant, an elf, or Elvis, and go out and party Austin-style!

Two doors down is local guitar hero Randy Franklin's **11** Yard Dog, an eclectic art gallery with a wide variety of work on display. Yard Dog opened in 1995 with a focus on folk art, and Franklin drove many miles through the South to acquire pieces from the likes of Mose Tolliver and Jimmy Lee Sudduth. Those artists, though both have passed, are still on the roster, but the gallery's range has expanded to include art by musicians such as Eric Bellis (Rico Bell), Jon Langford of the Mekons, and Austin singer-songwriter Bob Schneider. There's also some beautiful jewelry, particularly Nora Julia's earrings.

Look for the red boot and Western-style facade at the end of the block to find **12** Allen's Boots, which since 1977 has been the place to get Western wear. They carry boots in all the popular brands—Ariat, Lucchese, Justin, and Tony Lama—and while the vast array doesn't quite have the breathtaking beauty of the selection at Heritage Boots, these are a lot more affordable, and you can't go wrong with a pair of Luccheses. Allen's also carries Wrangler jeans and pearl-snap shirts to complete the classic look.

Across the street, the South Congress Hotel has only recently opened in what for many years was a parking lot. The hotel and its accompanying restaurants have taken SoCo to a previously undreamt-of level of luxury but are still too new to have really made their mark, and so for now we will pass them by.

Cross Monroe Street and pause to rummage through the treasures at **13** **South Congress Books**, in the middle of the next block. Sheri Tornatore opened her neat and impeccably curated shop in 2011. You will find rare editions, art, photography, and other quirky items in the rabbit hole of a store.

14 **Enoteca Vespaio**, serving Austin's best Italian food, is in fact two restaurants in one. They (mostly) share a menu, but more formal Vespaio is open only for dinner, whereas you can drop into Enoteca for a glass of wine and a salad anytime of day—if you can drag yourself past the case of fresh *dolci* at the front. It's a fun place to meet friends and people-watch, and we like to sit at the bar with a glass of red and the *bistecca con patate fritte,* the best version of the dish in town. Bonus pro tip: the restaurant has customer parking out back.

It's hard to pick a favorite from the array of stores in the next block. Candy store Big Top (billed as The Most Amazing Candy Shop the World Has Ever Known!) is always full, and a haircut at the Barber Shop is a classic Austin treat. But before you get to those, let's explore some cultural roots at **15** **Mi Casa Gallery**, a treasure trove of folk and religious art from Latin America. The store has a wonderful selection of Mexican *retablos,* or devotional paintings, a vast array of crosses from all over the world, and some beautiful Talavera pottery. It also smells wonderful, thanks to the signature home-blended citrus-spice potpourri, and of course you can buy a bag and bring the fragrance to your home.

June's All Day, mentioned earlier, is at the end of the block, but we are going to pop into Peg McCoy and Angela Atwood's **16** **Farm to Market Grocery**, an establishment that recalls the avenue's early days, when mom-and-pop bodegas sold eggs, sausage, and sugar to local residents. It's always a pleasure to browse the aisles of this sweet little store, where you can find staples and gourmet items, fresh flowers and chocolate, and always an abundance of neighborly kindness.

The final three items are all Austin classics, two of them more recent and the last, the first business of the SoCo renaissance. It was only in 2006 that Mike Rypka started **17** **Torchy's Tacos** in a trailer on South First Street. Now there are locations all over Texas and even in Oklahoma. As with Güero's, I don't think you can say you've been to Austin until you have eaten at Torchy's. They even have one at the airport. This South Congress store is the chain's mothership, so take your Dirty Sanchez and a grapefruit Jarritos to the patio and welcome yourself home. As the slogan proclaims, these tacos are "damn good." It's also no secret that Torchy's has a not-so-secret secret menu; order a Jack of Clubs or a Green Chile Pork Missionary Style and see what happens.

Torchy's is a good place to run into people, so perhaps you had better run across Mary Street to ⓲ Birds Barbershop for a "shortcut" before ordering your food. Both Torchy's and Birds were born in 2006—obviously a good year for Austin. Screenwriter Michael Portman and Wall Street trader Jayson Rapaport both quit their jobs and moved to Austin at the same time, starting Birds (apparently the name was supposed to attract women) to make "a small part of your day better and more affordable." With locations all over town (and one in Houston), Birds has become the quickest and most pleasant place to get a good cut. The stores are cool and fun: each features a different large exterior mural and is decorated with rock-and-roll swagger. Best of all, you can quaff a free beer while you wait for your stylist.

Our last port of call is an old-school Austin original a block south of Torchy's. The ⓳ Magnolia Cafe opened in this location in 1988 and has been serving omelets, coffee, and Mag Mud 24/8, as they put it, ever since then. The famous SORRY, WE'RE OPEN sign hangs on the door, the entrance to one of the friendliest vibes you'll ever encounter. It's old casual Austin at its best, and walking in the Magnolia is like taking a time machine straight back to the '90s, when every musician in town paid their rent chopping veggies or waiting tables here.

Points of Interest

❶ Heritage Boot Co. 1200 S. Congress Ave., 512-326-8577, heritageboot.com

❷ Blackmail 1202 S. Congress Ave., 512-804-5881, blackmailboutique.com

❸ Austin Motel 1220 S. Congress Ave., 512-441-1157, austinmotel.com

❹ Jo's Coffee 1300 S. Congress Ave., 512-444-3800, joscoffee.com

❺ Hotel San José 1316 S. Congress Ave., 512-444-7322, sanjosehotel.com

❻ Perla's 1400 S. Congress Ave., 512-291-7300, perlasaustin.com

❼ Service Menswear 1400 S. Congress Ave., Ste. A160; 512-447-7600; servicemenswear.com

❽ Hopdoddy Burger Bar 1400 S. Congress Ave., 512-243-7505, hopdoddy.com

❾ Güero's Taco Bar 1412 S. Congress Ave., 512-447-7688, guerostacobar.com

❿ Lucy in Disguise with Diamonds 1506 S. Congress Ave., 512-444-2002, lucyindisguise.com

⓫ Yard Dog 1510 S. Congress Ave., 512-912-1613, yarddog.com

⓬ Allen's Boots 1522 S. Congress Ave., 512-447-1413, allensboots.com

(continued on next page)

South Congress Avenue

(continued from previous page)

13 South Congress Books 1608 S. Congress Ave., 512-916-8882, southcongressbooks.com

14 Enoteca Vespaio 1610 S. Congress Ave., 512-441-7672, austinvespaio.com

15 Mi Casa Gallery 1700 S. Congress Ave., 512-707-9797, micasagallery.com

16 Farm to Market Grocery 1718 S. Congress Ave., fm1718.com

17 Torchy's Tacos 1822 S. Congress Ave., 512-916-9025, torchystacos.com

18 Birds Barbershop 1902 S. Congress Ave., 512-445-0500, birdsbarbershop.com

19 Magnolia Cafe 1920 S. Congress Ave., #3503; 512-445-0000; themagnoliacafe.com

28 Southern Walnut Creek Trail
A New Frontier

Above: A wild stretch of Walnut Creek

BOUNDARIES: Govalle Neighborhood Park, US 183, Johnny Morris Road, Daffan Gin Road
DISTANCE: Up to 15.4 miles out-and-back
DIFFICULTY: Easy to moderate, depending on the length of your walk
PARKING: Free parking at trailheads
PUBLIC TRANSIT: Govalle: Bus 300 to stop 5465; YMCA: Buses 237 and 339 to stop 6401; Austin
Tennis Center: Bus 233 to stop 6004; Daffan Lane: Bus 233 to stop 6005

There are many reasons to be thankful for Austin's congressman Lloyd Doggett, and this new trail is not far from the top of the list, as Doggett worked with BikeTexas to get $7 million of federal funding for this project. It opened in 2016 and in two years has steadily risen up the Austin outdoor charts, opening up parts of East Austin that have been historically neglected and connecting neighborhoods whose names many Austinites do not even know. It represents a major step forward in the recognition and preservation of the Boggy Creek and Walnut Creek watersheds. LIke the Northern Walnut Creek Trail and the Brushy Creek Regional Trail, this route is a park, a gym, and a community center and allows for a different outlook on the city. The wet woods and creekside flora that you will find along this trail are very different from the dry, rocky slopes of West Austin and the Hill Country. As you might expect, the trail's length and smooth curves and surface are like catnip to cyclists, but the 10-foot-wide concrete path is just as good for runners and walkers, who can enjoy the scenery at a more leisurely pace.

And scenic it certainly is, winding through a wonderland of dense woodland and grassy meadows, climbing leisurely hills, and dropping into green valleys, with every turn providing a new look at what still feels like a fresh discovery. The trail eventually climbs up to some fields at the top of Johnny Morris Road, providing far-reaching views of Austin along the way. As you walk, watch for cyclists who can't help but come quite fast down the inclines and around the smooth bends. They are almost always polite and respectful, so please play your part by keeping to the right side, and don't cross the trail without looking both ways. Not all the cyclists are Lycra-clad fanatics, and you will see plenty of family groups out and about. As the only interaction with cars is the quiet Jain Lane crossing, the trail is an excellent place to introduce children to the joys of cycling.

More wilderness on Walnut Creek

Walk Description

One of the main pros of the Southern Walnut Creek Trail is its straightforward nature. You don't have to follow a map or worry about which turn to take; all you do is follow the path, and walking this trail can be a meditative experience. There are regular distance markers to keep track of how far you have come and how far to the next landmark. When you've had enough, simply turn around and go back. There are four main trailheads, and you can also get to the trail at the junctions with Farm to Market Road 969 and Loyola Lane. For walkers it obviously makes sense to explore such a long route in separate sections, and it might be fun to return over a series of days until you have walked the whole length. For first-timers and visitors, it makes sense to start at the trail's beginning, at Govalle Park, and go to the US 183 bridge, for a 2.5-mile out-and-back walk.

From the trailhead, the concrete superhighway marches around the northern edge of the park, passing some grand pecan trees, and comes to the edge of Boggy Creek, which it then follows. This creek soon reaches the end of its 3-mile channelized section and wanders along a narrow ditch surrounded by the wide, grassy watercourse, bordered with a thick wall of woods. Walk through the small neighborhood around Jain Lane, with a detour onto the road bridge to take a look downstream. The trail then crosses over the Tannehill Branch and passes through the southern edge of East Boggy Creek Greenbelt. Just past the Tannehill bridge there is a dirt path leading into this practically unknown parcel of wilderness, should you want to stray from the concrete.

At the end of the greenbelt, there is another crossing, this time over the Fort Branch, and the trail follows rail tracks to go under the huge US 183 bridge. It then follows Delwau Lane 0.5 mile before veering north into the huge, multibranched Walnut Creek watershed. It continues another 2 miles through this previously inaccessible area to reach FM 969. From there the route follows Big Walnut Creek north to Loyola Lane and then climbs out of the valley up juniper-covered slopes to reach the flat fields at the trail's end. The most spectacular vistas are on this last section, though it is a mistake to single out any portion of the trail as particularly remarkable, because every step of the way is a delight.

The trailheads are listed on the next page. Begin at any of them and walk as long as you please, and you are sure to find some sweet vista or sun-dappled grove to brighten your day. This trail rivals any in the region for design, route, and natural beauty; it is safe for the whole family; and on most of its length you would not even know that you were in a city. The longer-term plan is to connect this trail with the Northern Walnut Creek Trail, though it will be some years into the next decade before that would be completed.

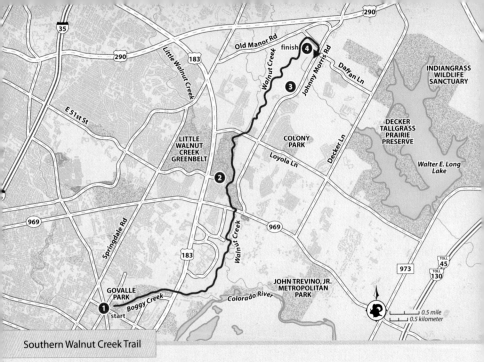

Southern Walnut Creek Trail

Point of Interest

Southern Walnut Creek Trail 512-974-6700, austintexas.gov/department/parks-and-recreation

Trailheads

1 Govalle Neighborhood Park 5200 Bolm Road

2 YMCA of Austin–East Communities YMCA 5315 Ed Bluestein Blvd.

3 Austin Tennis Center 7800 Johnny Morris Road

4 Johnny Morris Road Daffan Lane and Johnny Morris Road

29 Springdale Road
Galleries, Beer, and Bouldering

Above: *Find knickknacks and vintage clothing at Blackfeather Vintage Works.*

BOUNDARIES: Springdale Road from Airport Blvd. to Bolm Road
DISTANCE: 1 mile
DIFFICULTY: Easy
PARKING: Free parking on Springdale Road, at Canopy Austin, or behind Blackfeather Vintage
PUBLIC TRANSIT: Bus 300 to stop 5465

The Govalle neighborhood has been home to Mexican American families for many decades and is still a moderately low-cost area compared to other parts of Austin. The neighborhood has managed to retain a traditional family vibe while assimilating the influx of middle-class Anglos who are eagerly buying houses on the leafy streets around Govalle Avenue. The newcomers have brought change to the old industrial warehouses along the third of a mile of Springdale Road between Airport Boulevard and Boggy Creek, which are now home to galleries, breweries, workshops, and the largest rock-climbing gym in North America. We will browse some of these recently hatched ventures and introduce you to some of the owners and artists you might meet. Take this walk on a Saturday afternoon, and all of these locations will be open. Although the total distance covered is very little, plan on reserving at least a couple of hours to get the most out of each location. If you plan to go bouldering, wear athletic clothing.

Walk Description

Our first cluster of destinations is at the tip of the triangle between Airport and Springdale. Here we will find a vintage store, a contemporary art gallery, and the first stop, ❶ Ghost Pepper Glass, where you can watch or take glass-blowing classes or browse beautiful pieces like the peacock vases that I saw, all for sale and created by the staff. Owner Katie Plunkard first saw glass being blown in Malta at the age of 11. When she was finally able to try it herself 10 years later, she was hooked. Her impressive resume includes a period of study in Australia, and you can see examples from her *Urban Aviaries* series, small colorful birds inside transparent jars. Peek in at the workshop—circles of bright-orange heat blaze from gas-fired ovens. If you like what you see, sign up for an evening Taste of Glassblowing class, and take home your first creation. The studio is named for one of Plunkard's dogs, Ghost Pepper, who, together with fellow shop dog Dotti, hangs out at the studio to greet visitors.

Next door is ❷ Dimension Gallery, where a wrought iron fence with the most wonderful gate protects a fascinating and eclectic collection of sculpture, including Colin McIntyre's *The Resonant Lung,* a pipe organ sound chamber in a container. Colin works as a hot-metal forger, though recently he has become interested in working with hot tar. His large-scale works include the *Arboreal Passage* at the Austin Nature and Science Center and *Emergence* at the Houston Center for Contemporary Craft, and his pieces have been shown at the Ogden Museum of Southern Art in New Orleans, among many other places. Dimension is a collaboration with his wife, Moya, founder of Austin's Khabele School and the successful coworking space Vuka. After several shows featuring Colin's art, the couple decided that Austin lacked a home for sculptural artists and opened this gallery to support and encourage dimension in art. Associated artists include Nigerian-born Olaniyi Rasheed Akindiya, whose work explores moments in time and tensions between urban and rural life, and Peruvian ceramicist Alejandra Almuelle. Check the website for receptions and openings.

Moya McIntyre saw the empty service station behind Dimension and thought of pioneering Eastside entrepreneur Jessica Nieri, who was looking for a home for her latest project. Nieri fell in love with the bare warehouse walls and signed the lease, despite the amount of cleanup required to open a store there. ❸ Blackfeather Vintage Works showcases the lifelong collection of a friend of Nieri's who amassed an absorbing assortment of clothes and bric-a-brac. Prints, dresses, and jewelry crowd the space. Milwaukee native Nieri is no stranger to the area. She founded Café Mundi, one of the first wave of businesses on the Eastside, which in the '90s was a groundbreaking bohemian outpost on East Fifth Street where you could drink coffee among art to the sound of African music.

Leaving Blackfeather, walk south past the colorful Daily Greens facility into the next parking lot. This section of the warehouse has been refurbished, with large windows in place of steel shutters, and a handsome deck with a metal-and-wire fence. It's not that obvious from the outside, but this is the home of the ❹ Austin Bouldering Project, which is the largest rock-climbing gym in North America and has a schedule of yoga and fitness classes. Inside you'll find a whirl of activity and the chatter of excited children, as people move to and fro between the changing rooms and the huge climbing area. Anyone can sign a waiver and have a go. Climbing shoes are recommended, and you can rent them, but athletic shoes will work. The "boulders" are giant fake rocks, some 15 feet high, with handholds that present climbing challenges, all set on an enormous cushioned pad. It's a fun workout that is super popular with kids, and it is also a good way to get hungry. Austin Bouldering Project has you covered there: grab a healthy meal or snack from the Bento Picnic fridge to the right of the front desk.

You may also have worked up a thirst, so you will be glad that the next two places we will visit serve beverages. Turn left on exiting the Bouldering Project, and walk through a tall corridor to the other side of this building. Then turn right and follow the walkway back under a striking blue metal-and-glass awning. Look for the ❺ Austin Eastciders Collaboratory on the left. A visit to this taproom is a chance to sample the various delicious flavors of hard cider the brewery produces. Founder Ed Gibson is from Bristol in the United Kingdom, where cider made with apples from nearby Somerset has been the preferred tipple of locals for centuries. Beer lovers might want to pop into ❻ Friends and Allies Brewing Company next door and sample the large range of tempting brews, including the excellent Noisy Cricket IPA and the Urban Chicken Saison. They also serve nonalcoholic drinks like kombucha and cold-brew coffee. Founded in 2012 by Devon Ponds and Ben Sabin, the brewery aims to add an East Austin twist to West Coast brewing techniques. Take your drink outside and relax at a table, joining the lounging dogs and chatting people.

If you did not eat something from the Bento Picnic cooler, look in the parking lot for Maggie, ❼ The Ginger Armadillo food truck. At Maggie's window you can choose from a short but mouthwatering menu of what chef/owner Jen calls elevated Texas cuisine that includes items like brisket mac and cheese and Brussels slaw.

Leave the parking lot, walk south half a block, and then cross Springdale to reach ❽ **Canopy,** a community of artists and creators set in a collection of warehouses redesigned by the Michael Hsu Office of Architecture, whose work can be seen all over Austin. Walk into the compound and up the steps to the wide deck between two buildings. To the left, behind a heavy wooden door, is the ❾ **Big Medium Gallery.** Big Medium is a major supporter and promoter of contemporary art in Austin. They administer Canopy and put on important exhibitions like the Texas Biennial. They also run the tremendously successful East and West Austin Studio Tours that are such a big part of the city's art scene. In the gallery you will find new and interesting art from a wide range of Texas-based artists.

Next door is ❿ **Icosa Collective,** an artist-run contemporary gallery with 1,500 square feet of space whose internationally renowned members include photographer Leon Alesi and sculptor Terra Goolsby. It's an active community that puts on a wide range of shows and events.

Let's look at some of the items on display at the dual-use spaces in the building opposite. Walk past Sa-Tén (for the moment) and along the narrower deck that runs along the front of the old warehouse. These spaces combine a retail area and a workshop, so you can watch the art being made and talk to those involved in the creative process. The first stop is the studio of

The deck at Austin Bouldering Project

Backstory: Swedish Influence

Govalle is not a Spanish word; it is of Swedish origin and means "good grazing." Swante (or Swen) Swenson came to Texas in 1836, and at the urging of his friend Sam Houston, encouraged his countrymen to emigrate to Texas, which they did in large numbers, scattering odd words into the Texas lexicon. (His uncle, Sir Swante Palm, who also came to Texas and was promoted to vice consul for Norway and Sweden, was also instrumental in assisting this mass migration. See "Downtown," page 67, for more about him.)

11 Lisa Crowder, who moved her operation to Canopy in 2018. Her work primarily uses sterling silver and often consists of rough circles of metal combined into bold, wearable shapes that are highlighted with colored enamel. You might meet Crowder's assistant Sarah Heinzelman, who keeps the machine running and is a talented jeweler in her own right.

Next door is Steven Walker's **12** Modern Rocks Gallery, a must for music lovers. Walker, a Brit, was a touring guitar player who took up photography on the road and then managed a gallery in London before making his way to his dream city, Austin. Many of the prints feature classic British artists such as The Rolling Stones, The Clash, and The Beatles. Currently the gallery is displaying long-lost prints by Alec Byrne, who photographed the London music scene at the height of its glory, from the mid-'60s to the mid-'70s. Marvel at Byrne's photos of luminaries like Mick Jagger, Marc Bolan, and Pete Townshend in concert, in the studio, and simply hanging out. The gallery's other treasure trove is more local but just as iconic. You can still see Scott Newton photographing every *Austin City Limits* taping, as he has for decades, but he began his career at the Armadillo in the '70s, and some of his work from this golden period in Austin music is on display here.

At the end of this row, and your last chance to find a bargain or a present, is **13** Son of a Sailor. Owners William Knopp and Jessica Tata work mainly in leather, and the store features a popular collection of pet accessories. The name is a nod to William's time in the Navy, and originally their work had a more obvious nautical theme. Although there is a workshop here, the main manufacturing facility is in San Marcos.

Before you head back to your car, let's sit down for a moment and enjoy a perfectly poured coffee in the quiet Canopy location of **14** Sa-Tén Coffee & Eats. Give in to the temptation to sample a pastry or dig into a delicious Japanese-style lunch bowl or one of the all-day toasts.

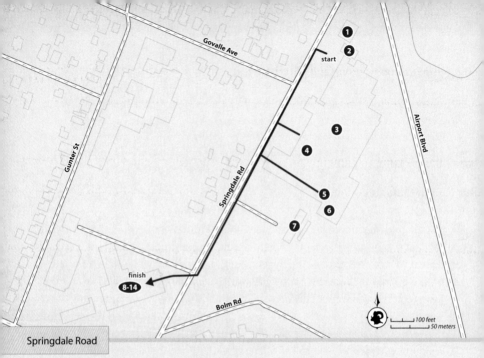

Springdale Road

Points of Interest

1 Ghost Pepper Glass 979 Springdale Road, #100; 512-766-5897; ghostpepperglass.com

2 Dimension Gallery 979 Springdale Road, #98; 512-479-9941; dimensiongallery.org

3 Blackfeather Vintage Works 979 Springdale Road, Ste. 98; 512-791-9372; blackfeathervintageworks.com

4 Austin Bouldering Project 979 Springdale Road, #150; 512-645-4633; austinboulderingproject.com

5 Austin Eastciders Collaboratory 979 Springdale Road, #130; austineastciders.com

6 Friends and Allies Brewing 979 Springdale Road, #124; friendsandallies.beer

7 The Ginger Armadillo info@thegingerarmadillo.com, thegingerarmadillo.com

8 Canopy 916 Springdale Road, 512-939-6665, canopyaustin.com

9 Big Medium Gallery 916 Springdale Road, Bldg. 2, #101; 512-939-6665; bigmedium.org

10 Icosa Collective 916 Springdale Road, Bldg. 2, #102; 512-920-2062; icosacollective.com

11 Lisa Crowder 916 Springdale Road, Bldg. 3, #102; 512-524-0364; lisacrowder.com

12 Modern Rocks Gallery 916 Springdale Road, Bldg. 3 #103; 512-524-1488; modernrocksgallery.com

13 Son of a Sailor 916 Springdale Road, Bldg. 3, #105; 512-524-0023; sonofasailor.co

14 Sa-Tén Coffee & Eats 916 Springdale Road, Bldg. 3, #101; 512-524-1544; sa-ten.com

30 Tejano Trails
Exploring *La Cultura*

Above: The Quintanilla House on East Cesar Chavez Street

BOUNDARIES: I-35, Lady Bird Lake, E. Third St., N. Pleasant Valley Road
DISTANCE: 4.9 miles
DIFFICULTY: Moderate, for length
PARKING: Limited free parking at Holly Shores; otherwise on the street
PUBLIC TRANSIT: Buses 4 and 300 to stop 1366

This walk co-opts most of the Tejano Walking Trail, a volunteer-led project from the East Cesar Chavez Neighborhood Planning Team that was six years in the making. The walking trail illuminates the area's journey from the post–Civil War expansion of the railroad to the 2009 dedication of a statue of labor leader César Chávez. We'll add some stops on the companion Trail of Tejano Music Legends and the northeastern portion of the Ann and Roy Butler Hike-and-Bike Trail along the lake. We'll stop at a restaurant or two where you can take a break. It's a rewarding and immersive journey in the rich culture of Austin's Eastside.

Walk Description

We begin at ❶ Holly Shores at Town Lake Metropolitan Park, on Canterbury Street at North Pleasant Valley. There are a few precious parking spaces here. Admire the Longhorn Dam, so named because the Chisholm Trail forded the Colorado River at this point. There's a small Chisholm Trail plaque on the dam confirming this next-level nugget of Austin trivia. The dam was completed in 1960, the last of the series along the Colorado. Like its upstream counterpart, Tom Miller Dam, it was built by the city and not the Lower Colorado River Authority (LCRA). Its unromantic and high-handed purpose was to turn the Colorado into a cooling lake for the old Holly Street Power Plant, which is now demolished.

We will follow the Ann and Roy Butler Hike-and-Bike Trail west along the lakeshore. (Read more about this trail and its founders in "Lady Bird Lake Boardwalks," page 110.) This northeastern section was the last section of the trail to be completed and has (like the Southern Walnut Creek Trail, page 149) opened up parts of East Austin that were previously unknown to most Austin residents. It's another example of the city's long-standing history of neglect and negation of the Mexican American community, a history that may be coming to a close, or at least nearing the end of a long chapter. The Tejano trail is a part of a new era of celebration of the community's culture and a way to remind everyone about this rich heritage that is both basic ingredient and added spice in the rich Austin *cazuela*.

Stop at the ❷ Roy Montelongo Scenic Overlook, visible from the parking area, which is the first stop on the Trail of Tejano Music Legends. With its concentric metal circles, the piece is an abstract of a spinning record, in honor of Montelongo's more than 20 releases. Raul Guerrero Montelongo was born in Hays County in 1938 and played saxophone from childhood on. He started his own band in 1964 and was a much-loved radio DJ with his own show, "¡Estamos en Tejas!" He died in 2001.

Follow the hike-and-bike trail west, crossing a bridge onto a long, narrow peninsula, a favorite of fishermen trying their luck in the quiet lagoon behind the spit of land. The trail doglegs around the site of the demolished power plant through Metz Neighborhood Park, which is often buzzing with the shouts of young men playing basketball. Holly Street Power Plant was seen as one of the city's most egregious examples of environmental racism, and one in a series of environmental injustices committed against East Austin that led to the 1991 formation of PODER (People Organized in the Defense of the Earth and her Resources), a group that is still active. The grassroots organization fought against the infamous Tank Farm chemical storage facility and against noise levels and pollution at the Holly Street plant. Their pressure finally led to Holly's closure in 2007.

Walk through the Aztec-looking portal at Holly Street, and turn right, looking for the matching arch on the south side of the street where the trail continues. Walk alongside the demolished plant past a wall on which the talented graffiti artists of the Eastside battle the city's overzealous cleaning efforts.

To your left is Manuel and Robert Donley Pocket Park. Multi-instrumentalist and composer Manuel "Cowboy" Donley was born in Durango, Mexico, and lived on Rainey Street (where Icenhauer's bar is now) until 1955, the same year he formed his band Las Estrellas, in which he merged rock-and-roll, bolero, and ranchera music into his own sophisticated and popular style.

Cross Riverview Street and walk past five baseball fields to arrive at a bridge over a channel leading to a large lagoon. In the corner of the lagoon is The Expedition School, where you can rent kayaks and stand-up paddleboards, from which you could explore Snake Island out in the middle of the lake at the end of Peace Point. The section of shore past the bridge is nicely and deliberately wild; it has been designated a nonmow area. Pass the boat ramp and continue along the trail, which goes along the shore through ❸ Edward Rendon Sr. Park at Festival Beach, site of music festivals and community gatherings large and small. Look for the statue called *Tenderly* to your right before the parking lot. It honors trumpeter and bandleader Ignacio "Nash" Hernández and is named for the hit he wrote for his wife. Nash was born in New Braunfels in 1922 and started the Nash Hernández Orchestra in 1949. Many Austin musicians, including Cowboy Donley, were members of this renowned group that mixed jazz and tropical sounds. The band is still gigging, though without its founder, who died in 1994.

From the statue, with the city skyline ahead of you, follow Nash Hernandez Sr. Road through the park to Comal Street, and turn right, heading north. Our next two stops are opposite each other before you reach Haskell Street. To the right is Sam Martin Middle School, opened in 1967 and named after a long-serving vocational teacher. After the war, this was the site of a soldier retraining center that burned down, leaving the empty lot on which the school was built. Sam Martin had (and has) white, black, and Hispanic students and was apparently built like a prison, with metal gates dividing the races. Opposite is a cul-de-sac called ❹ Robert Weaver Avenue, where low bungalows crouch under huge oak trees. These trees were a gift from President and Mrs. Lyndon Johnson, supposedly from their ranch in the Hill Country, and these little houses are a relic of a footnote in Austin's history that involved the president. The land south of Haskell Street and between Waller and Comal was once a fish hatchery, but after the dam was built, it became available for development, and in the late 1960s Johnson and other Texas politicians wrangled a piece of the hatchery land for a model neighborhood of low-cost homes. University of Texas social scientists took the time to study the feasibility of a mixed-race neighborhood and even had potential residents come in and look at scale models of the houses to see if different races required different floor plans. Some of the original 10 families—5 Mexican American and 5 African American, chosen from 300 applicants—still live here.

Walk back down Comal Street; turn right on Nash Hernandez Sr. Road and then right on Waller Street to look at the ❺ **Festival Beach Community Gardens**, where since 2010 some 80 gardeners maintain 10-by-20-foot plots. If you like the look of the gardens, volunteer for a community workday, held the second Saturday of every month. You might notice some unusual vegetables: the Multicultural Refugee Coalition's New Leaf Agriculture Program brings displaced farmers back to the land, and there are several Bhutanese and Burundian members who grow their traditional crops.

Continue north on Waller Street, crossing Holly Street and passing behind ❻ **Sanchez Elementary School.** The downtown section of I-35 was dedicated in 1962, literally setting into concrete the city's divide between east and west. Kids from East Austin had to cross the highway to get to Palm School (the sad old building at Cesar Chavez and I-35 that nobody knows what to do with), and so the community started advocating for a new school on the Eastside. With the help of long-term council member Gus Garcia, Sanchez Elementary was completed in 1976.

Turn right on Garden Street for a peek at the Floyd McGown House, two doors down at 1202, a two-story Victorian house, large for the neighborhood, that is on the National Register of Historic Places for its architectural interest. Return to Waller Street; turn right and then left onto Spence Street. You are in the tiny ❼ **Willow-Spence Historic District,** which includes Spence and Willow from west of San Marcos to Waller Street. The nomination file for the district cites the varied architectural styles—most houses are from the early 1900s up to 1930—with the bonus that this was a self-contained neighborhood with commercial buildings and stores. Walk down Spence to San Marcos Street, turn right, and return to Waller Street down the corresponding stretch of Willow Street. The trees that shade the quiet streets are as old as the houses themselves. This was originally an Anglo neighborhood, but the influx of Mexican families in the 1930s and the later construction of the interstate proved too much for the original inhabitants, who moved away. The isolated neighborhood declined, but the 1985 historic designation has been a game changer for this small community, as evidenced by the excellent condition of most of these lovely little cottages.

At Waller Street turn left and look for ❽ **El Buen Pastor Presbyterian Church** on the right. This church dates back to 1908, when Reverend Elias Treviño, a Presbyterian evangelist, came to Austin and founded the Iglesia Presbiteriana Mexicana at East Sixth and Navasota Streets. The church moved around some, changing its name to El Buen Pastor in 1951. The current attractive,

Mission-style building is from 1902, and the church acquired it in 1959. The sanctuary features stained glass, some brought from Germany and more than 100 years old.

Walk north to East Cesar Chavez Street, named after the legendary labor leader from Arizona, whose likeness can seen in the striking mural at Long Motors, across the street. Chávez is also memorialized in a statue at the **9** Henry S. Terrazas Branch Library, which is named for a young Austinite who lost his life fighting a forest fire while serving in the Marine Corps. The library was opened in 1976 and renovated and expanded in 2003 by Lawrence Group Architects of Austin.

Stop at the Cenote, kitty-corner to the library, for coffee drinks and tacos. Their patio is a fine place to pass a few restful moments before starting on the next section of this walk, which looks at four grand Victorian mansions along this street. These handsome homes, redolent of success, are a reminder of when the area first boomed, with the arrival of the railroad. The Houston and Texas Central reached Austin on Christmas Day in 1871, and crowds gathered to watch the last spike going in. The old Texaco warehouses on East Fourth Street at Waller are also survivors from this prosperous period.

Walk west to the end of the block to look at the **10** Evans-Morris-Hiesler House at 1000 E. Cesar Chavez St. This stunning mansion in the Queen Anne style was built in 1899 for George and Augusta Evans. Cross East Cesar Chavez and go east three blocks. Opposite Attayac Street is the **11** Moreland House, built for C. B. Moreland in 1897. The decorative gables and shingling are typical of the Queen Anne style common in houses of that era. Moreland was a painter whose work includes the star in the Texas Capitol rotunda, and the legend is that he used colors he had left over from other jobs. Keep east, cross Navasota, and look for the **12** Quintanilla House on the north side of the street, named not for the original owner but for Joel V. Quintanilla, who bought the property in 1972, intending to restore it, and earned the designation by risking his life to save a guest during the 1983 electrical fire at the Capitol. The solid-looking stone mansion features a two-tiered porch whose columns have very tall square plinths. The last house in this series of historic homes is the **13** Wolf House at 1602 E. Cesar Chavez, saved from destruction in 1974 and now an event center. This house also has a majestic two-tiered wraparound porch on its eastern side.

At this point you are probably ready for another break, so let's go east for just one more block, passing Los Huaraches and the Mission Funeral Home as we head for the colorful building at the Chalmers Avenue intersection, **14** Las Cazuelas Restaurant. This family-friendly eatery shows Mexican soap operas on the TV and serves a range of delicious Tex-Mex and Mexican dishes, including enchiladas, fajitas, and *huevos* every which way for breakfast. I am going to go out on a limb and say it's the best home-style Mexican cooking in Austin. But I must tell you that

Mission Hot Dogs behind Las Cazuelas serves bacon-wrapped hot dogs. Bacon or Tex-Mex? That might be the world's hardest culinary decision.

Walk north on Chalmers Avenue to the block between Third and Fourth Streets to see ⓯ **Chalmers Court Apartments**, another of Lyndon Johnson's projects, this one from his time as senator. These apartment buildings from 1939 are one of the first three public housing projects in the country. There were three because Chalmers was for whites, Santa Rita Courts at East Second and Corta was for Hispanics, and Rosewood Courts at East 12th and Chicon was for blacks.

Go east on East Third Street past the Pan American Neighborhood Park and Zavala Elementary. Turn right on Robert Martinez Jr. Street, and pause at ⓰ **Cristo Rey Catholic Church.** The grand limestone building is from 1959 and features a high handsome tower. César Chávez attended Mass here in 1973, after speaking to a small crowd during the United Farm Workers grape boycott of that year.

Walk down Robert Martinez Jr. Street and cross East Cesar Chavez and Willow Street, passing Metz Elementary, a bilingual school founded in 1916. Turn left at Canterbury Street to walk the five and half blocks back to Holly Shores, passing the north side of Metz Park.

Points of Interest

❶ Holly Shores at Town Lake Metropolitan Park 2711 Canterbury St.

❷ Roy Montelongo Scenic Overlook   At Holly Shores

❸ Edward Rendon Sr. Park at Festival Beach 2101 Jesse E. Segovia St.

❹ Robert Weaver Ave.

❺ Festival Beach Community Gardens 35 Waller St., 512-947-0882, festivalbeachgarden.com

❻ Sanchez Elementary School 73 San Marcos St.

❼ Willow-Spence Historic District Spence and San Marcos Sts.

❽ El Buen Pastor Presbyterian Church 1200 Willow St., 512-478-2221, elbuenpastorpc.org

Tejano Trails

31 Umlauf Sculpture Garden
Face-to-Face with Tenderness

Above: Diver *(1956) stands in perpetual motion at the edge of a pond.*

BOUNDARIES: Azie Morton Road, Barton Blvd., Barton Springs Road, Linscomb Ave.
DISTANCE: 0.2 mile
DIFFICULTY: Easy
PARKING: Limited parking at the museum; more across the street
PUBLIC TRANSIT: Bus 30 to stop 2144

Karl Julius Umlauf was born in 1911 in South Haven, Michigan, to German immigrant parents. His family suffered discrimination during the First World War, and Karl and his siblings anglicized their names. Eventually the family moved to Chicago, where Charles was able to attend a Saturday youth art program, having displayed his interest in form from an early age. His talent was recognized early on, and after graduating from Chicago's Austin High School, he studied at the Art Institute of Chicago with master sculptors Lorado Taft and Albin Polasek. He came to Austin in 1941 to teach at the University of Texas. Charles and his wife Angie loved Austin, and he stayed at UT, where Farrah Fawcett was one of his more famous students, until his retirement, gaining a reputation as a tough teacher but one who cared deeply about his students. He was known for his firm handshake and winning smile. The Umlaufs bought 2 acres above Barton Creek (for $2,800), and Charles set up his studio in the house on this property. Here the couple raised six children and many animals, and in this idyllic setting Umlauf was very prolific. In fact there are more pieces of his than of any other sculptor in public locations in Texas. His work can be found at the Witte Museum in San Antonio and the Houston Museum of Fine Arts, as well as the Smithsonian in Washington, D.C., and the Metropolitan Museum of Art in New York. His *Spirit of Flight* stands at Love Field in Dallas.

Charles was generous with his art, and over the years he gave dozens of sculptures to the city of Austin. In 1985 the Umlaufs donated their property to the city for use as a museum after their passing. Charles died in 1994, and Angie stayed in the house until her death in 2012. At one time the ponds on the 4 acres below the Umlaufs' promontory were used for fly-casting practice for soldiers but had become a wasteland used for dumping and covered in thick creepers. In 1991 the City of Austin took this abandoned lot and transformed it into a permanent home for the Umlaufs' bequest, and it is now managed by a private nonprofit organization in partnership with the city. There are nearly 60 pieces on display in the beautifully landscaped garden, and though these are all in bronze and stone, Charles worked in many different media, including wood and terra-cotta. His work is sensuous, lyrical, and profoundly tender about the human experience.

Walk Description

The ❶ Umlauf Sculpture Garden & Museum is set under the steep and wooded east bank of the Barton Creek valley, right below the Umlaufs' property. The entrance is on Azie Morton Road, and there are a number of pieces to enjoy in the small parking lot, including the two huge sets of concrete figures by the exit, *Mother and Child* and *Father and Son*. A breezeway takes you through the entrance building, where you must part with $5 to go farther and where there might be additional temporary exhibitions. Exit the building into the garden proper. A stream tumbles down the hillside and traverses the grounds to reach a lily-covered pond. Walk toward the hill to find the wide trail that goes up through the cedar elms to a vantage point at the top of the cascade. From here you can take in the sight of the whole grounds before you come back down to wander around the calm, tree-filled space—more arboretum than garden. It would be a lovely spot in which to while away a few minutes even without the art, but Umlauf's pieces transform the space into something much more contemplative and consoling. Start with *War Mother*, which is close to the entrance building and is one of the earliest pieces in the garden. It was made in 1939 as a response to the German invasion of Poland, and the response to this piece was what brought Umlauf to the attention of the University of Texas art department. Umlauf followed *War Mother* with *Refugees II,* and they are placed next to each other in the garden. But the *Weltschmerz* of these early works soon gives way to a more apolitical appreciation and celebration of humanity, and by the 1950s Umlauf had found his signature style. Most of the statues are of the human form in movement or reflection, and the pieces stand amid the native plants and gravel walkways as if waiting to come alive. *St. Francis with Birds* and two versions of *John the Baptist* emphasize the strong spiritual undercurrent in Umlauf's work. One section features animals, including a javelina and the popular *Lotus,* modeled after a hippo that lived in the San Antonio Zoo. *The Kiss,* Umlauf's dramatically sensual response to Auguste Rodin's *The Kiss,* is set in the center of the pond. *Diver* (modeled by Umlauf's son Arthur) stands at the bank, perpetually on the point of motion. All the bronze figures have been waxed to welcome inquiring fingers, and photography is encouraged.

Take your time to wander around the paths and pond, and let the art and the surroundings work their magic.

The Umlauf is also a leader in art education in the city, and they put on a host of programs, including the popular Umlauf After Dark series. There are concerts, talks, yoga, events, and openings. Parents, mark your calendars for Family Day, which is the second Sunday of every month. Eventually the museum will expand to include Umlauf's house and grounds at the top of the hill, where the sculptor's personal collection sits. Altogether, the Umlauf Sculpture Garden counts as one of Austin's most attractive features, combining art and nature within minutes of downtown.

This standing figure is one of the large statues that greet visitors.

Umlauf Sculpture Garden

Point of Interest

❶ Umlauf Sculpture Garden & Museum 605 Azie Morton Road, 512-445-5582, umlaufsculpture.org

32 The University of Texas
Architecture and Art

Above: UT's main building

BOUNDARIES: Nueces St., Speedway, MLK Jr. Blvd., W. 28th St.
DISTANCE: 2.5 miles
DIFFICULTY: Easy
PARKING: Street parking on Nueces and Rio Grande Sts.
PUBLIC TRANSIT: Bus 801 and 803 to stop 5864

Austin's heart still beats burnt orange, the instantly recognizable color of the University of Texas at Austin, which opened in 1883 with 221 students. The current campus was laid out in the 1930s by architect Paul Philippe Cret, and the university is defined by the orange roofs and enduring elegance of the original buildings, whose Spanish-Mediterranean style was thought, correctly, to suit the climate of Texas. This influential look still finds an echo in the Tuscan-looking architecture that is so prevalent in the Hill Country. Cret, a Frenchman from Lyon who came to America to teach at the

University of Pennsylvania, was a leading proponent of the maxims of the Beaux Arts school, and he used those principles to give the campus a feeling of balance and symmetry. To stroll through the grounds is to be immersed in his brilliant vision: the buildings emanate stability and erudition, and they somehow do this with a timeless lightness of touch, in calm contrast with the constant to-and-fro of the students and staff. This walk takes in the main section of the university and returns by way of Guadalupe Street (here known as the Drag) and the West Campus neighborhood. The free-and-easy atmosphere of the Drag of the last decades of the 20th century has mostly been replaced by an earnest studiousness. In between we will visit three of Austin's best museums.

Walk Description

We start at the graceful ❶ **Zeta Tau Alpha House**. This elegant neoclassical building with six columns was designed by Austin firm Page Southerland and built in 1939, and is a Texas Historical Landmark. Perhaps one of the most famous people to have stayed here is Lady Bird Johnson's daughter, Lynda Bird Johnson, whose presence required that the bedroom next door be converted into a command center for the Secret Service.

Walk south down Nueces Street and take the next left, West 27th Street. Cross Guadalupe on the south side of West 27th, where you might catch the scent of grilling from the In-N-Out Burger, and go one block to Whitis Avenue, passing the Phi Gamma Delta house across the street and stopping at ❷ **All Saints' Episcopal Church**. This church was built in 1899 as a chapel for Grace Hall, a women's residential hall. The hall was demolished, and the chapel became the parish church of All Saints'. It was built in 1899 with limestone from Liberty Hill, and from the west the tall entrance tower masks its length. Walk through the foyer at the bottom of the tower and into the church to admire the long nave, with its high arched ceiling and stained glass windows. All but one of these windows are by the renowned Willet Studios of Philadelphia, a business started in 1898 that is still going.

Go south on Whitis Avenue, passing Kinsolving Hall and the Belo Center for New Media. Cross busy Dean Keaton Street as part of the throng of students if school is in session. To your right is Building B of the Jesse H. Jones Communication Center, home for many years to tapings for *Austin City Limits*. Before you cross West 24th Street, look right at the grand ❸ **Littlefield House**, built in 1894 for Major George Washington Littlefield, Confederate soldier, banker, cattle baron, and major UT donor and booster. More about him later on this walk. His house is a grand and typically ornate Victorian mansion that "makes an imposing statement of wealth and privilege," according to UT professor and Page Southerland Page Fellow in Architecture Richard Cleary. One unusual feature is the Himalayan cedar in the front yard, imported from the Himalayas along with some Himalayan soil. The Littlefields had no children, and one can't help but think of the major and his wife, Alice, rattling around alone in this huge house. Alice left the house to the university when she died in 1935. Some say she was an unhappy woman—even that she went mad—and that her ghost still haunts the house. A statue of Barbara Jordan appraises you from the other side of West 24th Street The senator and civil rights leader taught ethics at UT after she retired from politics.

Enter the center of the campus, a nine-block area between 24th, 21st, Guadalupe, and Speedway. Follow Whitis Avenue to Inner Campus Drive, and pause in front of the ❹ UT Tower, part of the university's main building. The first main building, from 1899, is long demolished. New York architect Cass Gilbert—also from the Beaux Arts school—made several plans for a new campus in the early 1900s, and although none were implemented, he did design two buildings on the grounds, Sutton and Battle Halls. With these Gilbert defined the architectural style that Cret continued. Cret submitted his plan in 1933, which proposed four malls extending from a central building to serve as axes along which department buildings would be organized. After some back and forth, the university approved the plan and a design for the new main building, which included the 31-story tower that you see before you. When it was built, the tower was the only rival to the Capitol dome and, as Cret intended, has become "the image carried in our memory when we think of the place."

It was also the site of one of UT's darkest days. On August 1, 1966, Charles Whitman murdered his wife and mother, then made his way to the top of the tower, from which he shot 43 people over 96 minutes. Thirteen of his victims died. It was America's first mass murder in a public space, and the university took a long time to come to grips with the tragedy. Finally in 1999 they set up a memorial, which was replaced in 2016. Look for a stone plaque inscribed with the victims' names by the turtle pond in front of the tower.

Take the path to the right of the main building to come to the central courtyard, where the East, South, and West Malls meet. A statue of George Washington shares the uninterrupted view down the South Mall to the Capitol's granite dome. Behind you are the wide steps leading up to the main building's grand facade, and to your right, on the courtyard's western quarter, is the facade of Gilbert's ❺ Battle Hall, now the Architecture & Planning Library. ❺ Sutton Hall, is across West 22nd Street, past Parlin Hall. Look under the eaves and at the arched windows of the second floor; Gilbert's style is noticeably more decorative than Cret's, as you will notice if you walk along 22nd Street and compare Sutton to Parlin.

Walk south past Sutton Hall. The next building is the ❻ Harry Ransom Center, UT's research library. You would need to sign up for a research account and make a request to view such treasures as the Cardigan manuscript of Geoffrey Chaucer's *Canterbury Tales* or the 19th-century edition of Moses Roper's *A Narrative of the Adventures and Escape of Moses Roper, from American Slavery,* but casual visitors can inspect a Frida Kahlo self-portrait, a Gutenberg Bible from the 1450s, and the first photograph (yes, ever) and take in the always compelling temporary exhibitions. Ransom was an English professor who rose to the position of chancellor of the university system. He founded the Humanities Research Center, as it was known, in 1957, and became its director of special collections when he retired as chancellor.

From the Ransom Center, walk east, shadowing West 21st Street, a wide boulevard busy with determined-looking students rushing to the next class. Stop to marvel at the ➐ Littlefield Fountain, a World War I memorial in bronze and granite by Italian native and San Antonio resident Pompeo Coppini that was (finally) dedicated in 1933. The monument has been a lightning rod for controversy, as Major Littlefield had dedicated much of his life and fortune to "ensuring that the University of Texas was sufficiently branded as a South-centric institution." Coppini suggested the fountain as an alternative to an arch featuring statues of Confederate generals, which thankfully was too expensive even for Littlefield, though the statues were made and were originally clustered around the fountain. Cret had them moved to other locations on campus. In 2017 the UT administration removed several of them under cover of night. Coppini himself told Littlefield, "As time goes by, they will look to the Civil War as a blot on the pages of American history, and the Littlefield Memorial will be resented as keeping up the hatred between the Northern and Southern states."

Cross 21st and go east one block. Climb the short flight of steps leading to the plaza in front of the ➑ Perry-Castañeda Library, UT's main research library, open to the public and named for two former professors. Opened in 1977, this fine piece of brutalist architecture, apparently known as the book prison, is rhomboid-shaped and was designed by Phelps, Simmons and Garza and Associates of San Antonio, and Bartlett Cocke and Associates Inc. of Austin. The exterior is Indiana limestone, and the sheer facade looms over a slit of an entrance that could indeed lead into a jail. The side walls extend past the facade, giving the building a futuristic feel. Join the flow of people entering the building; the interior is much more welcoming, perhaps because here the walls are of Texas limestone. On the first floor, take a few minutes to browse the collection of more than 250,000 maps of different parts of the world, the library's most famous treasure.

Leaving the building, head south down Speedway. After a few steps, turn back for a different view of the arresting library. Here Speedway is a wide brick walkway leading to the ➒ Blanton Museum of Art. The main museum is the structure to your left, while the Edgar A. Smith Building to the right contains a café and meeting spaces. The first thing you will notice is Ellsworth Kelly's *Austin,* a white chapellike edifice. This iconic addition to campus is as significant as Donald Judd's buildings in Marfa or Houston's Rothko Chapel. As you have to go to the main gallery building to buy a ticket to enter the piece, we will visit the main collection first and return to the Kelly.

The Blanton's genesis was in 1994, when writer James Michener's wife, Mari, gave $5 million toward the construction of a new permanent home for the university art museum's scattered collection. The campaign got a boost in 1997 with a $12 million gift from Houston Endowment Inc., a generous enough contribution that the new facility was named for its chairman, Jack Blanton. Construction began in 2003, and the galleries opened with a grand celebration in 2006, as Austin rejoiced to join the ranks of cities with world-class museums.

The buildings were designed by Kallmann McKinnell & Wood Architects of Massachusetts, who were hired after the University Regents rejected more-adventurous plans from Swiss architects Herzog & de Meuron, a decision that caused a grand furor and the resignation of the dean of architecture. Herzog & de Meuron first proposed a complex with five flat roofs, then a delightful cushiony, curved design. Neither of these found favor, and the Blanton lost the chance to have a home as stunning as the collection. The current buildings echo and extend Cret's vision but make no strong architectural statement of their own. Nevertheless, the Blanton has some 18,000 pieces, including notable collections of Latin American, contemporary, and European art. Don't miss the paintings by Uruguayan Joaquín Torres-García and Cuban Wifredo Lam.

Procuring the Kelly chapel has made the Blanton a mandatory international art destination. This church of light was the artist's last work, and it is impossible not to see it as a response to Mark Rothko's Houston building. Both edifices use light to evoke spirituality, or at least an atmosphere of profound contemplation. Kelly, who lived in upstate New York, shared his generation of artists' fascination with Texas and its light, space, and mythos, and those elements are very much at play in this work.

More Texas mythos and swagger is on show across MLK Jr. Boulevard at the ❿ Bullock Texas State History Museum. There's an IMAX Theater, and in December 2018 the museum plans to open a revamped first-floor gallery called Becoming Texas, "a hands-on, immersive environment that uncovers Texas history with the most contemporary research on our past." The museum does an excellent job of presenting a fun, engaging, and educational narrative that ties all its exhibits into "the Story of Texas."

Cross MLK Jr. Boulevard and walk west, beginning the return leg. Pause at the bottom of University Avenue to take in the view up the South Mall to the main building and the tower. Pass the new McCombs School of Business at the corner of Guadalupe Street, where you will turn right onto the Drag, a corridor of bookshops and student eateries that during the semester is overrun with buses, cars, bikes, scooters, and pedestrians. Make your way past the striking limestone facade of St. Austin's Catholic Parish on the left and the Dobie Mall, sadly cleaned up from its former sleazy glory, to the right.

Cross to the west side of the street at West 21st, and take in Austin musician Daniel Johnston's famous *Hi How Are You* mural, featuring the art from his popular 1983 cassette release and available on T-shirts like the one worn by Kurt Cobain in 1992 at the MTV music awards. Continue north past the smell of Indian food from Teji's and in front of the Goodall Wooten Co-ed Dormitory, once the tallest building on the Drag and now overshadowed by the skyscraper apartment blocks that have taken over the skyline of West Campus.

Stop for a peek at the **⓫ University Baptist Church** sanctuary at 22nd and Guadalupe. Designed by Albert Kelsey, it was completed in 1921 to house a growing congregation and was added to the National Register of Historic Places in 1998. The vaulted ceiling has excellent acoustics, and the sanctuary has seen performances by Willie Nelson and Larry Gatlin, thanks to the church's connection with Gerald Mann, who became pastor here in 1973, served as Texas House and Senate chaplain, and went on to found the successful Riverbend Church by Lake Austin.

Turn left at 23rd Street into a pedestrian plaza with a grand mural of Texas. This square is home to the colorful Austin Arts Market, where local artists sell handmade jewelry, clothes, and scents. Walk through the market to get to our last stop, the **⓬ Gerhard-Schoch House**,

The Littlefield mansion on the grounds of UT

three blocks west. This 1887 house was the first two-story brick veneer house in Austin. Philip and Lena Gerhard had the house built and it passed to their daughter Clara and her husband, Dr. Eugene Paul Schoch, who taught chemical engineering at UT. The building stands in striking contrast to the new apartment blocks that surround it and is newly in great condition, thanks to the current owners, who bought the house in 2011 and began the process of renovation and preservation.

To finish our walk, go north three blocks on Nueces Street then right on block on 26th to **⓭ Kerbey Lane Café** on Guadalupe, one of the iconic Austin chain's seven locations, where you can enjoy a sandwich, a hamburger, or their famous Kerbey Queso.

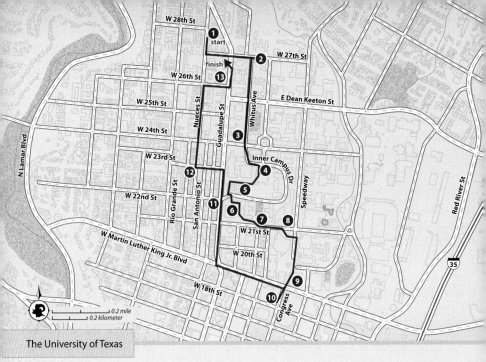

The University of Texas

Points of Interest

1 Zeta Tau Alpha House 2711 Nueces St.

2 All Saints' Episcopal Church 209 W. 27th St., 512-476-3589, allsaints-austin.org

3 Littlefield House 302 W. 24th St. (not open to the public)

4 UT Tower 110 Inner Campus Dr.

5 Battle Hall and Sutton Hall Inner Campus Dr.

6 Harry Ransom Center 300 W. 21st St., 512-471-8944, hrc.utexas.edu

7 Littlefield Fountain 201 W. 21st St.

8 Perry-Castañeda Library 101 E. 21st St., 512-495-4300, lib.utexas.edu/about/locations/pcl

9 Blanton Museum of Art 200 E. Martin Luther King Jr. Blvd., 512-471-5482, blantonmuseum.org

10 Bullock Texas State History Museum 1800 Congress Ave., 512-936-8746, thestoryoftexas.com

11 University Baptist Church 2130 Guadalupe St., 512-478-8559, ubcaustin.org

12 Gerhard-Schoch House 2212 Nueces St. (private residence)

13 Kerbey Lane Café 2606 Guadalupe St., 512-477-5717, kerbeylanecafe.com

33 Wild Basin Wilderness Preserve
A Hidden Cascade

Above: The waterfall at Wild Basin

BOUNDARIES: Capital of Texas Hwy., Bee Cave Road, Westlake Dr., Colorado River
DISTANCE: 1 mile
DIFFICULTY: Moderate
PARKING: At the preserve
PUBLIC TRANSIT: None

Operated as an educational resource by St. Edward's University, these 227 acres are a precious expanse of typical Hill Country terrain and topography within the city limits. The preserve exists because of the work of the environmental group Now or Never, who in the 1970s lobbied, rallied, and succeeded in raising enough money to purchase the tract. It is now part of the 24,000-acre Balcones Canyonlands Preserve and supports several threatened species, including our old friends the golden-cheeked warbler and black-capped vireo. The Wild Basin Creative Research

Center, affiliated with St. Edward's University, is located in a building on the preserve and facilitates research, public awareness, and preservation of Austin's wildlands. Print out the interpretive trail guide from the website before going, so you will know what to look for at the numbered and lettered signs along the Arroyo Vista and Creek Trails. With access to Bee Creek and grand vistas of the city and the wilderness, Wild Basin provides a scarce hour or two of escape and recharge. Please note that pets, bicycles, and picnics are not allowed in the preserve and that there is a $3 suggested donation for entrance. The terrain is steep and the trails rocky and often muddy and slippery, so dress appropriately.

Walk Description

The trails in the ❶ Wild Basin Wilderness Preserve make a series of widening triangles, starting with the short and easy Arroyo Vista Loop and ending with the Yaupon Trail, which scouts the hillside on the south side of Bee Creek. They cover the portion of the park that is open to casual visitors, a long promontory jutting southeast to overlook the creek valley. A deep canyon separates this part of the park from the peak that takes up the remainder of the area and that is off-limits to casual visitors. The larger triangles have some steep and rocky climbs down into and out of the thickly wooded Bee Creek gorge. This route takes you around the penultimate triangle, the base of which is the Creek Trail, which as the name suggests follows a branch of Bee Creek on its traverse of the southern part of the preserve toward the Colorado River. The Yaupon and Creek Trails come back together at a wide waterfall, which is situated where two branches of the creek come together and is hidden away in the wooded valley. Although this stream has the same name, it is a different Bee Creek from the one that flows through the city of Bee Cave to reach the Colorado at Inverness Point. This Bee Creek flows east through West Lake Hills and into Lake Austin just above Tom Miller Dam. You can see its mouth from Mozart's Coffee Shop or the Hula Hut on Exposition Boulevard.

The hike starts on the ridgetop and descends, as mentioned, to the rugged channel that runs east–west across the bottom end of the preserve. Take a picture of the map displayed at the trailhead to help you find your way around the trails. From this spot a short spur goes left to an observation point, where a bench offers a chance to take in the view across the steep, green valley. The main trail passes to the left of the Creative Research Center—a white house—and travels along a level gravel path through cedar and red oak. You will almost immediately come to the Arroyo Vista Loop. Here you go left. As the name implies, there are more great views of the wild arroyo on the northern side of the ridge. At the junction with the Triknee Trail, a detour leads left down some steps to an overlook, where you can read the information posted about the geology of the Hill Country and about the flora and fauna that live here. There are grand vistas of the rocky, green hills between the preserve and the Colorado River. The overlook trail takes you back to the Triknee, where you turn left and start down a long series of wide steps in the direction of the creek valley. The scrubby juniper around you echoes with the sharp tweets and trills of cardinals and other birds.

Keep left, moving on to the Possum Trail, which continues down yet more steps. The woods get thicker and the shade gets deeper as you descend. To your left you will see the feeder creek from the arroyo flowing down a deep trench. The path doubles back on itself at the beginning of the Creek Trail. Pass the first Yaupon junction and then cross Bee Creek on stepping-stones. Climb up from the creek to a junction where a short spur to the right leads to a scenic view. This part of the preserve along the valley is always pretty magical, especially if there has been rain. A thick tangle of trunks, branches, and briars cloaks the rocky streambed, and although you are less than a mile from Loop 360, you are at the same time in a Hill Country valley that could be far away. Eventually you will come to the falls, where the stream tumbles off a limestone ledge into

a deep, shaded pool. Walk up the other end of the Yaupon Trail a few yards to come to the top of the waterfall. Follow the Warbler (or Falls) Trail to begin the 0.5-mile climb back to the trailhead. Steep steps lead up the side of the spur. Keep left to join the Laurel Trail and again to follow the other side of the Arroyo Vista Loop back to the research center and the trailhead.

If you want to learn more about the flora, fauna, and geology of the preserve, consider joining one of the Second Saturday Guided Hikes, a two-hour guided hike with naturalist John Barr. Visit the website to sign up for the quarterly eBird walk, when volunteers record the bird species they hear or see along the trails and enter them into the eBird citizen science database.

Another view of the waterfall

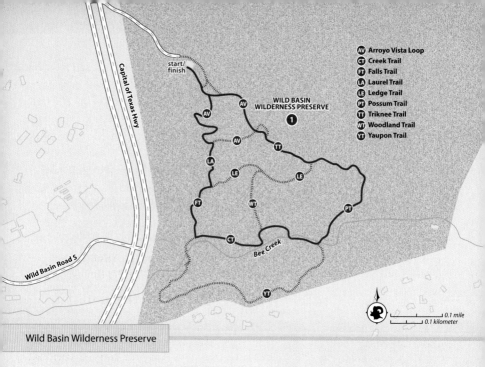

Wild Basin Wilderness Preserve

AV Arroyo Vista Loop
CT Creek Trail
FT Falls Trail
LA Laurel Trail
LE Ledge Trail
PT Possum Trail
TT Triknee Trail
WT Woodland Trail
YT Yaupon Trail

WILD BASIN
WILDERNESS PRESERVE
1

start/
finish

Capital of Texas Hwy

Wild Basin Road S

Bee Creek

0.1 mile
0.1 kilometer

Point of Interest

1 Wild Basin Wilderness Preserve 805 N. Capital of Texas Hwy., 512-327-7622, wildbasin.org

Appendix: Walks by Theme

Nature Hikes

Barton Creek Greenbelt (Walk 4)
Blunn Creek Nature Preserve Trail (Walk 6)
Brushy Creek Regional Trail (Walk 9)
Goat Cave Karst Nature Preserve (Walk 15)
Hornsby Bend (Walk 16)
Inga's Trail at Bull Creek Greenbelt (Walk 18)
Red Bud Isle Trail (Walk 25)
Shoal Creek Greenbelt (Walk 26)
Southern Walnut Creek Trail (Walk 28)
Wild Basin Wilderness Preserve (Walk 33)

Neighborhoods

Bouldin (Walk 8)*
Crestview (Walk 11)*
Hyde Park (Walk 17)*

Shopping & Nightlife

East Sixth Street (Walk 14)*
South Congress Avenue (Walk 27)*
Springdale Road (Walk 29)*

Culture & History

Austin's Mexico (Walk 1)*
Austin's Music Landmarks (Walks 2 and 3)*
Clarksville (Walk 10)*
Downtown (Walk 12)*
East Austin (Walk 13)*
Tejano Trails (Walk 30)*
The University of Texas (Walk 32)*

Parks

Blunn Creek Greenbelt (Walk 5)
Boggy Creek Greenbelt (Walk 7)
Lady Bird Johnson Wildflower Center (Walk 19)
Lady Bird Lake Boardwalks (Walk 20)
Mary Moore Searight Metropolitan Park
  (Walk 21)
Mayfield Preserve Garden (Walk 22)
Northern Walnut Creek Trail (Walk 23)
Onion Creek Loop at McKinney Falls (Walk 24)
Umlauf Sculpture Garden (Walk 31)

* Scooter/bike friendly

Brushy Creek Lake (see Walk 9, page 47)

Index